How To Succeed
in Law School

By E. Scott Fruehwald

Table of Contents

Preface

You have bought this book either because you are struggling in law school or because you are worried how you will do in law school. The good news is that there are proven learning techniques that will help you succeed in law school. This book will introduce you to them.

Last year, I wrote a book that showed law professors how they could help their students succeed.[1] This book turns that book around to show you how you can use these techniques to succeed in law school.[2]

Over the last twenty years, there has been a major revolution in how cognitive scientists understand how the brain works and how it learns. (I will discuss this revolution throughout this book.) These scientists and educational researchers have used these insights to determine which learning techniques are most effective and which are almost worthless. Unfortunately, they have discovered that most learning methods used by college and law students, such as rote learning, rereading, and passively attending classes, are ineffective and inefficient. However, they have also discovered and widely tested techniques that will help you succeed in your learning endeavors. These techniques include active learning, self-testing, spaced studying, interleaving, and many, many more.

These techniques are what this book is about. There are three fundamental steps to succeeding in law school:

1. Adopt a growth mindset.
2. Adopt the most effective learning and studying techniques.
3. Work hard.

I will talk about all three of these in depth in this book. In particular, I will present in detail the most effective learning and studying techniques for law students.

I. The Developmental Stages of Learning.

The first question is where do you want to be when you finish law school? Do you want to graduate at the top of your class or just make it through? Do you want to get a good job, or will just any job do? To understand the answers to these questions, you need to understand the developmental stages of learning.

Succeeding in law school involves attaining the proper stage of learning–the self-authoring stage. This book's purpose is to get you to that stage. Learning does not stop in the late adolescence stage, but extends into adulthood.[3] (Law students are adult learners.) There are five stages of learning:

- First stage: impulsive
- Second stage: instrumental
- Third stage: socializing
- Fourth stage: self-authoring
- Fifth stage: self-transforming.[4]

The first stage, "impulsive," is a "position of childhood."[5] (I hope you left this stage long ago.) The second stage, "the instrumental way of knowing," "is the ability to see a reality beyond one's own perception or vantage point."[6] While individuals at this level can control their impulses and needs, they cannot create abstractions from their observations,[7] and their thinking tends to be black and white.[8] They hold a relatively fixed concept of self, and they view others as aids or obstacles in fulfillment of the self.[9] In other words, they have an instrumental or utilitarian way of knowing related to their self-interests.[10]

Students in this stage look to their teachers for knowledge in order to advance their careers and other self-interests.[11] They consider knowledge absolute and want detailed teaching from their teachers.[12] 10% of all individuals remain in this stage, and about 68% of students enter college in this stage.[13] (Think about friends or classmates who were in this stage. Did they have difficulty learning? Were you at this stage when you entered college? Have you advanced beyond this stage?)

With the third stage, the "socialized way of knowing," individuals can undertake abstract thinking and deal with the theoretical.[14] This order stresses social identity–"the self is no longer the only 'set or category' (as in the more concrete second order), but a person can instead 'experience the self in relation to a . . . set or category.'"[15] In this order, a person "can internalize both the individual's own viewpoint and that of another person, and can make self-reflective decisions based on the interaction of these viewpoints."[16] Significantly, individuals "can 'subordinate their needs and desires to the needs and desires of other people.'"[17] Authority is knowledge.[18] Thus, this is a socialization stage–"education is pursued to "meet the goals and expectations of external authorities . . . and/or valued others.'"[19] Because of this, students can perceive criticism as an attack on their self-worth within the group, instead of constructive criticism.[20] (Responding to constructive criticism is vital to effective learning.) Most adults are in this stage.[21] Most law students graduate in this stage. (Think about friends or classmates who were in this stage. How did this affect their learning? Are you currently in this stage? If you are it is okay, unless you do not want to advance beyond this stage.)

Critics often attack American legal education because it creates third stage socialization, which is a type of social constructivism.[22] These critics claim that law schools turn out cookie-cutter attorneys who think alike, making law school a socialization process, rather than a developmental process. (Do you want to be a cookie-cutter attorney? Which is more important development or socialization?)

Scholars criticize social construction educational approaches as romanticizing the community and not preparing students "to critically examine the community's values, practices, and beliefs."[23] (This is an important part of being a lawyer.) The danger is that this stage fails to help individuals "perceive limits in the dominant paradigms of the day or to perceive conflict between those paradigms and more fundamental values."[24] Stated similarly, "Membership in these communities does not include an ability to stand apart from the community and appreciate that membership in a community can sometimes involve blindness to the community's evils."[25] As one author has noted, "this epistemology does not empower students with a capacity to reflect on how lawyers think—in sum, to move beyond the socializing values of the third order of consciousness."[26] It certainly does not create lawyers who are capable of becoming self-engaged, self-directed thinkers.

The fourth stage is the "self-author[ing]" way of making meaning, with only about one-half to one-third of adults reaching this stage.[27] At this level, "knowledge is no longer the property of external authorities or experts; instead, it is constructed 'through experience, reflection, [and] analysis,' informed by thoughtful use of 'teacher, texts, [and] authorities.'"[28] (Don't you want to be able to do this?) In this stage, identity is separate from the social context, and "individuals at the fourth order can take perspective and reflect on their roles within social contexts and systems."[29] At this level, "learners balance varying points of view and learn to see value in the process of understanding and (at times) reconciling areas of commonality and difference."[30] Those at this stage can "self-define as a professional with a moral core of responsibility and service to others."[31] In other words, "lawyers and law students who function at the fourth order have the capacity to critically reflect on the legal system as a whole and on their own interaction with and role in the system."[32] Individuals at this level can "make systematic critiques of the law by observing both how numerous aspects of the legal system interact with each other and from observing the moral reasoning that takes place as the values of the legal system <u>interact with their own personal values</u>."[33] Individuals at this stage can change the discourse. This is the stage I want you to achieve in law school.

II. What This Book Will Do for You.

The early chapters of this book will introduce you to the basics of learning the law, the second part will give you the tools you need to become a self-authoring learner, and the final part will tell you things you need to know about law school.

Chapter One shows you had to adjust your attitude to become a better learner. It will discuss the growth mindset, which you must have to succeed at anything. Simply stated, if you think you will fail, you will. Second, it will demonstrate how you can motivate yourself. If you are not motivated, how can you succeed? Finally, it will help you adopt the best attitude to law school, which is also necessary for success.

Chapter Two is probably the most important chapter in the book because it explains how to study effectively. Students with good study habits succeed in law school; those who don't have good study habits do poorly or fail. This chapter will show how your study habits from high school and college have hindered your learning. More importantly, it will give you the study techniques that you can use to succeed in law school.

Chapter Three teaches you how to read legal texts. It will discuss effective reading in general, then it will teach you how to analyze (brief cases). The final part of this chapter will introduce you to the five types of legal reasoning and how to identify them in legal opinions.

Chapter Four begins to introduce more advanced concepts, which will help you succeed in law school. This chapter will explain "metacognition." I realize you may have not heard of this term before, but it is thinking about thinking. Metacognition helps you control your thinking processes, and it leads to more effective learning.

Chapter Five discusses self-regulated (or self-directed learning). This chapter will help you achieve stage four from above–self-authoring. Most successful law students can learn on their own, and self-regulated learning is vital for lawyers because the law is complex and constantly changing.

Preface

Chapter Six tells you the details of what to expect in law school, such as information about doctrinal classes, exams, legal writing, legal research, summer jobs, etc.

Chapter Seven gives you essential context for attending law school. When I went to law school, we were given a one-hour class on case briefing, then thrown into the pool. It is better today, but you still need more context than you get on orientation to be ready for your first day of classes.

Chapter Eight talks about the important topic of law school wellness. Law school is very stressful, and you need to know how to deal with its everyday stresses. There are professionals at all law schools who can provide needed help.

You will find many exercises throughout this book. Most of these exercises are reflection exercises; they make you think about yourself and how you learn. It is important that you do these exercises; reflection is a key to deep learning.

Ready to move on. Let's start with the growth mindset in Chapter One.

Notes

1. E. Scott Fruehwald, How To Grow A Lawyer: A Guide for Law Schools, Law Professors, and Law Students (2018).

2. If you are a law student buy this book. If you are a law professor or law school administrator, buy the other one.

3. Michael J. Cedrone, *The Developmental Path of the Lawyer*, 41 Cap. U. L. Rev. 779, 803-21 (2013); *see generally* Robert Kegan, In Over Our Heads: The Mental Demands of Modern Life (1994).

4. Cedrone, *supra* at 810; Neil W. Hamilton & Verna Monson, *Legal Education's Ethical Challenge: Empirical Research on How Most Effectively to Foster Each Students Professional Formation (Professionalism)*, 9 St. Thomas L. Rev. 325, 337 (2011). Of course, there are overlaps in these categories, and all adults are not at the same stage of development. Benjamin V. Madison III, *The Emperor has No Clothes but Does Anyone Really Care? How Law Schools are Failing to Develop Students' Professional Identities and Practical Reasoning*, http://papers.ssrn.com/sol3/papers.cfm?abstract_id=2414015 at 35 (2014). I will not deal with the fifth stage, the self-transforming stage because it "is mostly theoretical and ordinarily reached only after midlife, if at all." Cedrone, *supra* at 810.

5. Cedrone, *supra* at 810.

6. *Id.* at 811.

7. *Id.* at 812.

8. Hamilton & Monson, *supra* at 337.

9. Cedrone, *supra* at 812.

10. *Id.*

11. *Id.*

12. *Id.*

13. *Id.* at 811-12.

14. *Id.* at 814.

15. *Id.*

16. *Id.* at 814-15.

17. *Id.* at 815.

18. *Id.*

19. *Id.*

20. *Id.* at 816.

21. Hamilton & Monson, *supra* at 337.

22. Cedrone, *supra* at 816-818.

23. *Id.* at 817.

24. *Id.* at 818.

25. *Id.*

26. *Id.*

27. *Id.*

28. *Id.* at 819.

29. *Id.*

30. *Id.* at 827.

31. Hamilton & Monson, *supra* at 337.

32. Cedrone, *supra* at 819

33. *Id.* at 820. (Emphasis added)

Chapter One
Adjust Your Attitude

Chapter Goals.

1. To help you understand the growth mindset.
2. To show you how to develop a growth mindset.
3. To help you understand motivation.
4. To help you understand how to motivate yourself.
5. To help you understand cognitive motivators and emotional motivators.
6. To help you understand the importance of setting goals.
7. To help you understand the differences between learning goals and performance goals.
8. To help you understand the difference between intrinsic and extrinsic motivation.
9. To help you understand self-efficacy.
10. To help you understand the importance of a supportive environment with motivation.
11. To show you how to create the subjective value of the goal.
12. To show you how to create the expectation for successful achievement of the goal.
13. To show you how to create a positive learning environment.
14. To show you how you can regulate your emotions for self-motivation.
15. To show you the importance of taking charge of your learning.
16. To show you the importance of developing the right attitude toward law school.

The first thing you need to do before you start law school is to adjust your attitude. You have to convince yourself that you can succeed in law school, you must motivate yourself to work hard, and you must adopt the right attitude toward law school.

I. Adopt a Fixed Mindset.

If you don't think you will succeed, you won't.[1] This seems self-evident, but many students entering law school think they can't succeed. They want to be lawyers. They've dreamed of being lawyers all their lives. But now that they've made it to law school, they think they can't do well.

Professionals call this the fixed mindset.[2] With the fixed mindset,

1

students think that intelligence is fixed. " No matter what I do I can't do any better." As one professor has declared, "[d]efeated students do not believe that they have the cognitive ability to succeed. In other words, they experience a loss of hope."[3]

Recent research has demonstrated that the fixed mindset is a myth.[4] With the proper approach and hard work, students of average ability can improve their intelligence. For example, one study "found that eight 25-minute classes for seventh graders focused on the message that 'learning changes the brain by forming new connections and that students are in charge of this process' led to increased classroom motivation and reversed a decline in grades experienced by the control group."[5] In other words, intelligence is fluid or malleable. This is called the growth mindset, and it is "based on the belief that your basic qualities are things you can cultivate through your efforts."[6]

The growth mindset is based on the discovery that intelligence is both nature (genetics) and nurture (experience and learning).[7] You can increase your intelligence through hard work. Let me repeat that: you can increase your intelligence through hard work. In fact, this author believes that any student who can get into law school can succeed if they adopt the growth mindset and employ the learning techniques set out in this book.

What are the advantages of having a growth mindset? Researchers have shown that students who believe that intelligence is malleable get higher grades than those who don't.[8] This is a simple fact, and doesn't it make sense, even without any research? Remember the childhood story of the little train that could. "I think I can. I think I can."

How do you change from a fixed mindset to a growth one? Much of this book is devoted to doing this, but I will give you a general introduction here.

1. You must believe that you can improve your intelligence through hard work. This may be difficult to do, but as one writer has declared, "[m]indsets are beliefs. They're powerful beliefs, but they're just something in your mind, and you can change your mind."[9] Think of your role models, and how they achieved success. Did they have a fixed mindset? No, they had a "just do it" mindset. If you are having trouble changing your mindset, read one of the books on the growth mindset, such as Carol S. Dweck, Mindset: The New Psychology of Success (2006), or look for growth mindset articles on the internet. I bet you will find hundreds of articles on the growth mindset.

2. Improve your learning and study techniques. Poor learning and study techniques help create the fixed mindset because they lead to failure. Effective learning and study techniques lead to the growth mindset because they lead to success. You probably use poor learning and study techniques because no one has ever taught you how to learn and study. This book is intended to change this. (See especially Chapter Two)

3. Think about how you have succeeded in your life. You must have had some successes if you made it to law school. Think in detail about these successes. Did they involve hard work? Did they involve taking the right approach? How did you get good grades in undergraduate school. Did the teacher just like you, or was it something else? Most applicants don't get accepted to law school. Why did you get accepted, while others didn't?

4. Talk to people who have succeeded in their field. Did they have a fixed mindset or a growth mindset? Were they just lucky, or was it something else?

5. Understand how learning works. I deal with this in depth later in this book, but for now you need to understand that some learning approaches are effective, while others are not. This is based on how the brain learns. For example, "Human neurobiology is elastic, which means that students have the capacity to generate new neurons, synapses, and retrieval pathways, thereby increasing their working memories, long-term memories, and the pathways that give them access to the memories. Thus, students' learning capacities are malleable."[10] In other words, understanding how the mind works shows how intelligence can be increased, thus, supporting the growth mindset.

There are other dangers from the fixed mindset. First, you must understand that failure is part of learning–that even the greatest thinkers failed before they achieved success.[11] If you have the fixed mindset, you will believe that failure confirms your inability to learn. On the other hand, if you have the growth mindset, you will realize that failure leads to learning and success. As one writer has noted, "[t]hose with the growth mindset kept on learning. Not worried about measuring–or protecting–their fixed abilities, they looked directly at their mistakes, used the feedback, and altered their strategies accordingly."[12] Or, as another scholar has declared, "The question becomes 'How smart do you want to be?' not 'How smart are you?'."[13]

The above is especially true for first-year law students. First-year law students have generally succeeded at their educational undertakings, but, when they get to law school, they start to struggle and make lots of mistakes. They even make mistakes when they talk in class, and they are unable to deal with the embarrassment because they have always said intelligent things in class and received praise. <u>It is important to understand that law school is hard.</u> <u>Everyone struggles.</u> Everyone! (The first time I was called on in Contracts, I gave a really stupid answer to a basic point. I graduated number two in my class.)

Another problem is when a student with a fixed mindset gets good grades in high school or college. Students often come to law school over-confident because of the emphasis on self-esteem in public school teaching ("Everybody gets a trophy.").[14] Because of this, poorer students usually have more problems seeing their lack of skills than better students.[15]

But, even better students can suffer from a fixed mindset. Because they have succeeded easily in the past, they do not think that they have to work harder now. However, because law school is much more difficult than most college majors, it requires hard work even from students who were highly-successful in the past. In addition, when such a student receives a poor grade, that student will often attribute it to inaccurate grading or prejudice from the teacher, rather than the fact that the student didn't work hard enough or took the wrong approach.[16] Thus, the student will not change her approach or work harder.[17]

Finally, <u>you should be wary of false praise</u>. Many times teachers, parents, and others praise your work when it really isn't very good. This is especially true of parents who love their children and want them to succeed. False praise can lead to a fixed mindset if you accept it uncritically. We all like praise, but it is important to understand how we are really doing.

Exercises

1. What is the fixed mindset?
2. What is a growth mindset?
3. Do you generally have a fixed or a growth mindset?
4. Do you have a fixed mindset in some areas, but a growth mindset in others? Why do you have a fixed mindset in certain fields?
5. Why is the fixed mindset bad?
6. What are the dangers of a fixed mindset?
7. How can the fixed mindset affect student learning?
8. How can a fixed mindset hurt good students? How does false praise affect you?

9. How does law school affect students' mindsets?
10. How can you overcome a fixed mindset? (Do this exercise even if you do not think you have a fixed mindset.)
11. Do you learn from your mistakes?

Exercises

1. Sit back in a comfortable chair and reflect on your life. How did you get where you are? How did you do in elementary school? Were you a good or poor student? Why? How do you do in high school? Were you a good or bad student? Why? Did you succeed in some classes, but not others? Why? How did you do in college? Were you a good student or a bad student? Why? Did you succeed in some classes, but not others? Why?
2. Think about your favorite athlete? Do you think that he or she has a fixed mindset? Do you think an athlete with a fixed mindset can succeed?
3. Think about your friends in high school and college. Which ones succeeded and which ones failed? How did your friends talk about their successes and failures? How does this match up with their mindsets?
4. When you failed at something who did you blame? Your teachers? Your parents? Were you right? How did this relate to a fixed mindset?
5. How do you deal with mistakes? Making mistakes is an essential part of learning, but many students are embarrassed when they make mistakes. Law school is more difficult than college, and you will make lots of mistakes. Your classmates will make lots of mistakes, too. If you adopt a positive attitude to making mistakes, you will learn more, feel better about yourself, and help develop a growth mindset. It is not important how many times you stumble; it is important how you finish.
6. Think how famous people made mistakes? Did they learn from their mistakes? How did they end up?
7. Has there been a time in your life when you thought you received too much praise? How did this affect you? Did you work harder or less? How did this affect your mindset?

II. Motivate Yourself.

If you are not motivated to do the work required by law school, you will fail in law school or, at least, be at the bottom of the class. This is another obvious fact. However, law school requires a great deal of reading of complex and difficult material. You must motivate yourself to do the work.

How to Succeed in Law School

A. The Theory Behind Motivation

Let me start with the boring scientific basis of motivation, then I will give you practical advice on how to motivate yourself. Don't skip the boring part. Understanding how motivation works helps you motivate yourself.

Motivation is "the personal investment that an individual has in reaching a desired state or outcome."[18] "Motivation is the psychological construct that is used to describe those things that impel and sustain us in putting forth effort."[19] It is "the general answer to the question of 'why' we do what we do, especially why we do things that are hard to do."[20] It "is not a stable trait of an individual, but is more situated, contextual, and domain specific."[21] Finally, motivation involves "[your] choice of activities, the intensity of [your] effort or level of cognitive engagement within those activities, and [your] persistence at those activities."[22]

There are two types of learning motivators: cognitive motivators and emotional motivators.[23] Cognitive motivators include "needs for the self, for recognition, achievement, esteem, respect, and confidence."[24]

Setting goals is the most important cognitive motivator because motivation is goal-directed.[25] You achieve a goal when you value that goal and expect to attain that goal as a result of your actions.[26] When you set your goal, you exert "cognitive effort" to achieve your goal.[27] Setting goals directs your attention on that goal (helps you focus on your goal).

The most important type of goal for creating motivation for law school success is learning goals, which are "goals directed at learning new knowledge or mastering a task or problem."[28] With learning goals, you concentrate on competence and the inherent facets of a task, learning for learning's sake, interest, challenge, and curiosity.[29]

In the past, you probably concentrated on performance goals ("goals directed at demonstrating ability or doing especially well in relation to others."), such as grades, or task goals (regarding assignments "as tasks to complete rather than opportunities to learn"), or even work avoidance goals (getting "through with as little time and effort as possible").[30] Students who have performance goals want to protect their self-image, to acquire status, recognition, and praise by appearing competent and intelligent.[31] When students with performance goals do not receive positive external feedback, they can become anxious, apathetic, or depressed, and they often adopt procrastination.[32] (Does any of this sound familiar?) Work avoidance goals are very bad. Students with work-avoidance goals are trying to avoid looking incompetent, hold little interest in learning, and seem disengaged or alienated.[33] You might have a work-avoidance goal in one class, but a learning goal in another class you are more engaged in.[34] (Does this sound familiar? Which classes did you do better in?)

There is also intrinsic and extrinsic motivation, which are similar to learning goals and performance goals, respectively. Motivation to learn for its own sake is intrinsic, while motivation as a means to an end is mainly extrinsic.[35] "Intrinsic motivation taps into the natural human tendency to pursue interests and exercise capabilities."[36] It involves autonomy, competence, and relatedness (and hard work).[37] Intrinsic motivation is better for learning because students who attribute success to internal causes are more likely to succeed.[38] On the other hand, extrinsic motivation includes things like praise, getting good grades, and rewards, and it is not as effective as intrinsic motivation.[39] Motivation for an activity can be both intrinsic and extrinsic. Most importantly, "law student unhappiness occurs when students ignore the internal signals of 'meaning' in work and instead focus on extrinsic goals."[40]

Three factors affect whether goals are motivating: 1) the subjective value of the goal, 2) the expectation for successful achievement of the goal ("expectancies"), and 3) whether the environment is supportive or unsupportive ("the environmental context").[41]

First, whether a goal is motivating depends on its value to you ("how much the goal is worth"), and how it compares to other goals.[42] Values are subjective and personal because humans learn to value things that engender positive emotions.[43] There are three types of value goals. First is attainment value, "which represents the satisfaction that one gains from mastery and accomplishment of a goal or task."[44] An example of attainment value is when a person devotes many hours to chess to master the game. The second value is intrinsic value, "which represents the satisfaction that one gains from simply doing the task rather than from a particular outcome from a task."[45] An example of this value is when a person learns the cello just because they enjoy it. Finally, instrumental value "represents the degree to which an activity or goal helps one accomplish other important goals, such as gaining what are usually referred to as extrinsic rewards."[46] Examples include studying economics to become a better lawyer or getting an M.B.A. at night to obtain a raise at work.

The second motivating factor–the expectation for successful achievement of the goal–comprises two parts: 1) outcome expectancies ("the belief a specific action will bring about the desired outcome") and 2) efficacy expectancies ("the belief that one is capable of identifying, organizing, initiating, and executing a course of action that will bring about the desired outcome").[47] A positive outcome expectancy might be "if I work hard in this course I will get a good grade." A negative outcome expectancy, such as "no matter how hard I work in this class, I will get a C," can have significant consequences on a student's motivation, causing that student to give up.[48]

Connecting short-term goals with long-term goals can also create positive outcome expectancies.[49] For example, one might complete a home-work assignment in French class to help attain the goal of learning French. Similarly, one might learn French to help that individual obtain a legal job in Paris. A group of scholars has described one method of incrementally deve-loping long-term goals: "(1) envisioning possible futures for themselves, (2) conceptualizing those futures as goals, (3) construing a path for goal obtainment, (4) making explicit connections between present educational activities and the valued future goals, (5) discussing possible roadblocks and forks in the path, (6) brainstorming strategies for managing imagined future obstacles, and (7) interviewing successful adults from the community about their own strategies for reaching goals."[50]

Efficacy expectations (or self-efficacy) are vital for motivation be-cause they "affect human functioning by influencing the extent to which people are optimistic versus pessimistic, make resilient versus detrimental attributions for successes and failures, apply appropriate coping strategies for dealing with difficult situations, and persist in the face of challenges."[51] In other words, efficacy expectations are important because "[s]tudents will not set and pursue a goal unless they feel confident that they can do what is needed to achieve it."[52] In contrast, students with high self-efficacy tend to be more engaged, work harder, and achieve more, as well as take harder cour-ses.[53] Self-efficacy can be conscious or unconscious, and students can have high self-efficacy in some areas but not others.[54]

Efficacy expectations come mainly from a student's past successes ("mastery experiences") and failures.[55] "When students successfully achieve a goal and attribute their success to internal causes (for example, their own talents or abilities) or to controllable causes (for example, their own efforts or persistence) they are more likely to expect future success."[56] Efficacy ex-pectations can also be obtained vicariously by observing others succeed and receive praise.[57] Other factors influencing efficacy expectations include: "(1) the student's current skill level, (2) the extent to which she has witnessed modeling from peers and teachers. . ., (3) verbal persuasion regarding the difficulty of the task, and (4) the student's current psychological state."[58] Negative efficacy expectations, (such as "last time I succeed by luck" or "I never will become a better student") can be particular damaging to motivation.[59]

It is important that self-efficacy be accurate.[60] As mentioned above, inaccurate praise is meaningless, and, will eventually hurt self-efficacy.[61] Similarly, teachers should make sure that tasks and assignments are achievable.[62]

The final factor in motivating students through goals is whether the environment is supportive or unsupportive.[63] (Of course, you may have little control over this one.) Ingredients of this factor are "the complex dynamics of the classroom, its tone, the interpersonal forces at play, and the nature and structure of communication patterns. . ."[64] An unsupporting environment can damage motivation, even in the presence of positive factors on the other elements.[65]

One can summarize the elements of successful learning goals as follows:

I. The subjective value of the goal,
    A. Attainment value,
    B. Intrinsic value,
    C. Instrumental value.
II. The expectation for successful achievement of the goal,
    A. Outcome expectations,
    B. Efficacy expectations,
III. Whether the environment is supportive or unsupportive.

There are also emotional motivators. Emotional motivators, which are biological, involve pleasure and pain.[66] Positive emotions help focus attention; individuals sustain effort and maintain capacity.[67] Negative emotions produce avoidance, such as avoiding a task that an individual thinks she is not good at (lack of self-efficacy).[68]

Interest (situational and personal) is a motivator that is usually associated with emotion, although it can have cognitive elements, too.[69] Situational interest comes from the environment, is produced by novelty ("sensory features that appear to draw our attention"), is generally based on positive emotions, and can be short- or long-term.[70] You can create situational interest by approaching learning in novel and exciting ways. (I will give you some suggestions later in this book.) On the other hand, personal interest (or curiosity) derives from our experiences.[71] It helps individuals work to long-term goals and helps sustain attention and persistence.[72] As I will state several times throughout this book, developing your curiosity is the most important factor in becoming a successful student.

How you attributes success can also affect your motivation.[73] You are more likely to be motivated and succeed if you attributes success to controllable internal factors, like effort (a growth mindset).[74] On the other hand, if you attribute success or failure to external factors (a fixed mindset), such as luck, favoritism, or someone else, you destroy motivation.[75]

Exercises

1. What is motivation?
2. How do cognitive motivators differ from emotional motivators?
3. Why is goal-setting important in motivation?
4. What are learning goals? What are performance goals? Which type is more important for effective learning?
5. What is the difference between intrinsic and extrinsic motivation? How do they relate to learning goals and performance goals?
6. What affects whether goals are motivating?
7. Why is the value of a goal important to its achievement?
8. What is the difference between outcome expectations and efficacy expectations?
9. Where do efficacy expectations come from?
10. How does high self-efficacy help students learn?
11. What are negative efficacy expectations?
12. How does self-efficacy relate to the growth mindset?
13. Why does self-efficacy have to be accurate?
14. How does the environment affect motivation?
15. What is the role of emotion in motivation?
16. What is interest in connection with motivation?
17. Now that you understand how motivation works, can you think of some ways you can help motivate yourself? Also think how you would motivate others if you were the teacher.

B. Practical Motivation

Now that we're done with the boring part, let's discuss how you can motivate yourself. You can increase your motivation by 1) creating the sub--jective value of the goal, 2) creating the expectation for successful achievement of the goal, and 3) creating a positive learning environment. (Reread the last sentence until you have it memorized.)

Start with a goal. Goals can include "I will learn Torts" or "I will learn how to play the violin." "I will write an excellent paper for legal writing class." "I will get a summer job." Make your goal as clear and detailed as possible.

Next, you want to create the subjective value for the goal. (Subjective means personal to you.) Preferably this will be a learning goal. Ask "what will I get from this goal"? To make it a learning goal, try to be curious about the goal. ("I want to learn about criminal procedure because I want to be a criminal lawyer.") Also, think about what accomplishing the goal will do for you. ("If I learn French this semester, I can study in Paris this summer.") Think how this goal will help with long-term goals. ("If I learn calculous, I can study advanced physics.")

Many of your law school goals will relate to your courses. Before each course, think about what the course covers. In other words, do a little advanced reading. Then, from the syllabus and first class, try to determine what your professor is trying to accomplish with the course. Then, ask "what is my goal for the course?" Ask "how will this course help me in the future?" "What course is this course a building block for?" (Property is the foundation for wills and trusts, real estate transactions, and land use regulation.) You can also set goals for each individual class. "What do I want to get out of today's class?" Thinking like the above will help motivate you for the class.

You also need to set goals for studying. Students are not motivated for studying by aimless study sessions. "What do I need to study tonight?" "What do I want to accomplish through this study session?" (I will discuss studying in detail in the next chapter.)

You must also motivate yourself to learn skills. Law school is not just memorizing facts; it is also analyzing legal materials and applying your knowledge. Miniskills that are important for law school include deductive reasoning, inductive reasoning (*e.g.*, synthesizing cases), analogical reasoning, distinguishing cases, and making policy arguments. Practical skills include writing litigation documents, drafting documents, such as contracts and wills, making oral arguments, negotiations, and trial practice. As you learn the above skills, think how they will help you become a lawyer.

Setting long-term goals is also important. Here is a plan for creating long-term learning goals:

> First, individuals must establish an ideal self
> and a personal vision for the future (i.e.,

Who do you want to be?), which is based on developing an image of a desired future, fostering hope that one can achieve their goals, and identifying established strengths upon which the personal vision can be realized. Second, they must identify their "real self," which includes an honest assessment of strengths and weaknesses, and then compare it to their ideal self, or who they want to become. Third, they must devise a tailored learning plan, which establishes a set of personal standards that the individual needs to meet to "close the gap" between their real self and their ideal self. Fourth, they need to engage in activities that allow them to experiment or practice with new behaviors, thoughts, feelings, or perceptions. And finally, they must develop and maintain close, personal relationships with people who can help them move through these steps and toward their goal of realizing change.[76]

You must also create the expectation that you will successfully achieve your goal. You must develop self-efficacy–that intellectual abilities are changeable if you use the sufficient effort and proper methods ("a growth mindset"), rather than unchangeable ("a fixed mindset").[77] (I discussed self-efficacy in detail above.) Focusing on learning goals, rather than performance goals, helps your self-efficacy because with learning goals achievement is measured against past performance and, thus, failure is less traumatic than when students have performance goals, such as getting a good grade or status.[78] You should frame "problems as surmountable and as a chance to practice and demonstrate specific skills, rather than threatening or barriers to success."[79]

You can also regulate your self-efficacy through self-efficacy self-talk," where "[s]tudents engage in thoughts or subvocal statements aimed at influencing their efficacy for an ongoing academic task."[80] Such statements can include "You can learn to ski" or "You can complete this will drafting assignment." In fact, a recent study has shown that athletes that encourage themselves in the second person ("you") are more likely to triumph.[81]

You should also allow yourself opportunities to reflect.[82] Reflection from prior learning affects subsequent learning, particularly self-efficacy.[83] Reflection also helps you become invested in what you are doing, and it makes learning more interesting.

A final part of creating motivation is creating a favorable learning environment. Unfortunately, much of this is controlled by your law school and professors. However, there are a few things you can do to improve your learning environment. First, in class, concentrate. Do not surf the net, text friends, or stare out the window. The human mind has limited attention, and doing things other than learning wastes attention. Next, when studying, find a quiet place where you can concentrate without being disturbed. Turn off all electronic devices because they will divert your attention from learning.

Here are a few more details on how you can motivate yourself. First, you can use "self-consequating," which involves providing consequences for your behavior.[84] These are extrinsic reinforcements or punishments, such as "after I do this assignment I will have a cup of tea" or "if I don't finish the brief this afternoon, I can't go to the movie tonight."[85] Self-praise upon completing a task is another example of self-consequating.[86] A second type of controlling motivation is "goal-oriented self-talk"; "students using goal-oriented self-talk think about or make salient various reasons they have for persisting or completing a task."[87] This type can relate to learning goals, performance goals, or task goals.[88] For example, a goal for self-talk might be learning how to play the Mozart clarinet concerto or getting a good grade for finishing an assignment. A third method is "interest enhancement," in which "students [] use strategies designed to increase their immediate enjoyment or the situational interest they experience while completing an activity," particularly with boring or repetitive tasks.[89] An example of interest enhancement is making studying a game.[90] Finally, students can use "environmental structuring," which is reducing distractions or increasing readiness for studying by changing location or avoiding activities like eating and drinking.[91] Other examples of environmental structuring include keeping a schedule calendar or allocating specific times each day to studying.[92]

Students can also affect their motivation by regulating their emotions so that they can exert the effort to complete a task.[93] It is especially important for students to control negative emotions, such as negative self-talk and test anxiety, because they can affect outcome and self-efficacy expectations.[94] One strategy to overcome negative emotions is self-talk, such as "You arte not going to compare yourself to your classmates" or "You worry too much; You are progressing in finishing this task."[95]

Finally, the most important factor is to take charge of your learning. When you are in charge of your learning, you will be motivated. (I will talk about self-regulated learning in a later chapter.)

Exercises

1. Think about a paper you had difficulty writing in college? Would writing the paper have been easier if you had been more motivated? How could you have motivated yourself to write that paper better?
2. Do you set goals when you do a task or take a course? Do you see how setting goals can help you do better in that class? Think about a class you did not do well in in college? What goals could you have set for that class?
3. Did you set learning goals in college? Can you see why they are more effective for motivation than other types of goals? Think about a paper you did poorly on in college, and how learning goals could have helped you with that paper?
4. Do students who learn for learning's sake do better than other students in college?
5. Think about a class you did well in in college. What was the subjective value for that course for you?
6. Think about how a class you took in college helped you in a later class? Can you see the importance of long-term goals?
7. What were your long-term goals for college? Did you accomplish them?
8. When you undertake a task, do you consider whether your approach will help you achieve your goal?
9. When you undertake a task, do you consider how well you can do that task? (Is the growth mindset relevant here?)
10. Do you draw on past successes to help you set efficacy expectations for the future?
11. Did you think about your learning environment when you were in college? Were there any ways you could have improved your learning environment in college?
12. Have you ever used emotional motivators? Think of a college class you could have done better in if you had used emotional motivators?
13. When you learn something, do you view it as a task or as something new you can learn (novelty)? Can you see how adopting a novelty approach could help your learning?
14. Think about a hard project you want to do. Think how you can create the

expectancy of creating that project?

15. Do you use self-consequating? What self-consequating things do you think will be successful for you?

16. How can you use interest enhancement to help motivate you to study?

17. Do you try to reduce distractions while studying?

18. Do you have negative emotions about learning? How can you reduce these negative emotions?

19. Do you take charge of your learning, or do you expect others to take charge of your learning? Are you an active or passive learner?

20. Why are you going to law school? What are your long-term goals for law school?

21. Why did you pick your particular law school? Did your choice relate to learning?

22. Create a mission statement for your law school career, your legal career, your life.

III. Your Attitude To Law School

Finally, you need to develop the right attitude toward law school. It should be obvious from the above that if you don't have the right attitude toward law school you will not do well.

The wrong reasons for going to law school:

1. I don't have anything better to do.

2. There's a recession on, and I can hide in law school.

3. I really like this television program about the law. (When I went to law school, L.A. Law had just become a big hit. A lot of my classmates went to law school because of L.A. Law.) (Don't expect the law to be like tv or the movies.)

4. Uncle Jack said I should go to law school.

5. My parents expect me to go to law school.

6. I hear you can make a lot of money being a lawyer.

The right reasons to go to law school:

1. I want to be a lawyer, and I've researched what lawyers do.

2. I want a job that I can use to support my family, and I researched what lawyers do.

15

3. I want to help people. (Of course, this one probably means that you won't make a lot of money, but it can lead to personal satisfaction.)
4. I admire lawyers I know, and I want to be like them.
5. The law fascinates me.

In addition to going to law school for the right reasons, you must also have the right attitude towards law school. You must be willing to work hard. You must be willing to face challenges. You must be eager to learn new things. You must be eager to learn new skills. You must be eager to learn new ways of learning. You must be ready to change yourself. You must be ready to become a professional.

Exercises

1. Why do you want to go to law school? Are your reason(s) among the good reasons above?
2. If you have a bad reason to go to law school, do you also have a good reason?
3. Are you ready to take on everything law school involves?

Wrap-Up Exercise

What are the two most important pieces of advice I gave you in this chapter?[96]

Notes

1. As a leading expert in this field has stated, "[t]he view you adopt for yourself profoundly affects the way you lead your life." CAROL S. DWECK, MINDSET: THE NEW PSYCHOLOGY OF SUCCESS 6 (2006)

2. *Id.*

3. Robin S. Wellford-Slocum, *The Law School Faculty Conference: Towards a Transformative Learning Experience*, 45 S. TEX. L. REV. 255, 269 (2004).

4. Dweek, *supra.* at 7.

5. *Id.*

6. *Id.*

7. DANIEL T. WILLINGHAM, WHY DON'T STUDENTS LIKE SCHOOL? 4 (2009).

8. *Id.* at 180. Professor Dweck relates that a mindset workshop had a significant impact on students' learning and grades. DWECK, *supra* at 215 ("This one adjustment of students' beliefs seemed to unleash the brain power and inspire them to work and achieve.").

9. DWECK, *supra* at 16.

10. Jeffrey J. Minneti, *A Comprehensive Approach to Law School Access Admissions*, 18 U. MARY. L. J. RACE, RELIGION, GENDER & CLASS 189, 198 (2018).

11. WILLINGHAM, *supra* at 184.

12. DWECK, *supra* at 111.

13. Minetti, *supra* at 198.

14. Karen McDonald Henning & Julia Belian, *If You Give a Mouse a Cookie: Increasing Assessments and Individual Feedback in Law School Classes*, 95 U. DET. MERCY L. REV. 35, 45-47 (2018).

15. *Id.*

16. SUSAN A. AMBROSE ET.AL., HOW LEARNING WORKS: 7 RESEARCH-BASED PRINCIPLES FOR SMART TEACHING 201 (Jossey Bass 2010).

17. *Id.*

18. AMBROSE, *supra* at 68.

19. DUANE F. SHELL ET.AL., THE UNIFIED LEARNING MODEL: HOW MOTIVATIONAL, COGNITIVE, AND NEURO-BIOLOGICAL SCIENCES INFORM BEST TEACHING PRACTICES 14 (2010).

20. *Id.*

21. Elizabeth A. Linnenbrink & Paul R. Pintrich, *Motivation as an Enabler for Academic Success*, 31 SCHOOL PSYCH. REV. 313, 314 (2002).

22. Christopher A. Wolters, *Regulation of Motivation: Evaluating an Underemphasized Aspect of Self-Regulated Learning*, 38 EDUC. PSYCH. 189, 190 (2003).

23. SHELL, at 68.

24. *Id.*

25. *Id.* at 69-71; *see also* AMBROSE, *supra* at 70-71 ("[G]oals serve as the basic organizing feature of motivated behavior.").

26. Shawn M. Glynn et.al., *Motivation to Learn in General Education Programs*, 54 J. GEN. ED. 150, 158 (2005). [http://jesserbishop.wiki.westga.edu/file/view/ motivation%20general%20education.pdf]

27. SHELL, *supra* at 69.

28. *Id.* at 118-121; *see also* AMBROSE, *supra* at 72 (The students truly want to learn.); Linnenbrink, *supra* at 320-21.

29. Judith L. Meece et.al., *Classroom Goal Structure, Student Motivation, and Academic Achievement*, 57 ANN. REV. PSYCH. 487, 490 (2006). [http:// tu-dresden.de/die_tu_dresden/fakultaeten/fakultaet_mathematik_und_naturwissenschaften/fa chrichtung_psychologie/i4/lehrlern/lehre/diplom/lehrveranstaltungen/lehren_lernen/annurev. psych.Goal_Meece2005.pdf]

30. SHELL, *supra* at 118; Linnenbrink, *supra* at 320-21.

31. AMBROSE, *supra* at 71; Glynn, *supra* at 159.

32. Glynn, *supra* at 159; Paul R. Pintrich, *Motivation and Classroom Learning, in* 2 HANDBOOK OF PSYCHOLOGY at 110 (2003). [hereinafter Pintrich, *Motivation*]

33. AMBROSE, *supra* at 72; Linnenbrink, *supra* at 321.

34. AMBROSE, *supra* at 72-73.

35. Glynn,. *supra* at 156.

36. *Id.*

37. R.A. Kusurkar et.al., Motivation as an Independent and a Dependent Variable in Medical Education:A Review of the Literature, 33 MEDICAL TEACHER 242, 243 (2011) [http:// www.intrinsicmotivation.net/SDT/documents/2011Kusurkar_ReviewMedEduc.pdf]. The authors added, "The need for autonomy or self-determination is related to the feeling of volition in one's actions. The need for competence is related to one's feelings of capability in achieving the target. The need for relatedness concerns the desire to relate to the significant others in one's life through work and achievement." *Id.*

38. Pintrich, *Motivation, supra* at 107.

39. *Id.* Professors Hanning and Belian have observed that many students consider law school a commodity. Hanning & Belian, *supra* at 43. I have seen many students like this in my 15 years of teaching, and they rarely do well in law school.

40. Larry O. Natt Gantt II & Benjamin V. Madison III, *Self-Directedness and Professional Formation: Connecting Two Critical Concepts in Legal Education*, 14 U. ST. THOMAS L.J. 498, 510 (2018).

41. AMBROSE, *supra* at 70-82. This approach is usually called "the expectancy-value model," and it is grounded in social cognitive theory. Pintrich, *Motivation*, *supra* at 105.

42. AMBROSE, *supra* at 74; SHELL, *supra* at 70.

43. SHELL, *supra* at 71.

44. AMBROSE, *supra* at 75.

45. *Id.*

46. *Id.*

47. *Id.* at 76-77.

48. *Id.* at 77.

49. *Id.* at 124-126.

50. *Id.* at 125.

51. George M. Slavich & Philip G. Zimbardo, *Transformational Teaching: Theoretical Underpinnings, Basic Principles, and Core Methods,* ED. PSYCH. REV. 560, 578 (2010) [http://ted.coe.wayne.edu/ed7999/Transformational.pdf]; *see also* Albert Bandura & Edwin A. Locke, *Negative Self-Efficacy and Goal Effects Revisited*, 88 J. Applied Psych. 87, 87 (2003). [http://projects.ict.usc.edu/itw/gel/BanduraLockeSE-Goals.pdf]. Self-efficacy is distinguishable from self-esteem in that self-efficacy is situated and contextualized (task specific), while self-esteem is more general. Linnenbrink, *supra* at 315.

52. SHELL, *supra* at 126; *see also* Bandura & Locke, *supra* at 87 ("Whatever other factors serve as guides and motivators, they are rooted in the core belief that one has the power to produce desired effects; otherwise, one has little incentive to act or to persevere in the face of difficulties.").

53. Linnenbink, *supra* at 315.

54. Wolters, *supra* at 191; Glynn, *supra* at 161.

55. SHELL, *supra* at 127; Glynn, *supra* at 161.

56. AMBROSE, *supra* at 78.

57. Slavich & Zimbardo, *supra* at 578; SHELL, *supra* at 127.

58. Schwartz, *Teaching Law Students*, *supra* at 456.

59. AMBROSE, *supra* at 78; SHELL, *supra* at 121 ("[S]tudents are not likely to set goals unless they believe they can achieve them.").

60. Linnenbrink, *supra* at 316.

61. *Id.*

62. *Id.*

63. AMBROSE, *supra* at 79-82.

64. *Id.* at 79.

65. *Id.* at 79-82.

66. SHELL, *supra* at 76

67. *Id.*

68. *Id.* at 77.

69. SHELL, *supra* at 78-80; *see also* Linnenbrink, *supra* at 318 ("interest in general is defined as the interaction between the individual and his or her environment.").

70. SHELL, *supra* at 78-79; Glynn, *supra* at 155; Linnenbrink, *supra* at 319.

71. *Id.* at 80; Glynn, *supra* at 155 ("Students . . . who are interested or curious about topics are oriented toward inquiry and discovery. . ."); Linnenbrink, *supra* at 319.

72. SHELL, *supra* at 80.

73. Linnenbrink, *supra* at 317.

74. *Id.*

75. *Id.*

76. Slavich & Zimbardo, *supra* at 579.

77. *See also Id.* at 589. The is also been phrased in terms of whether a student has control over his or her learning. Pintrich, *Motivation, supra* at 106 ("This self-determination perspective is crucial in intrinsic motivation theories of motivation in which students are only intrinsically motivated if they feel autonomous and their behavior is self-determined rather than controlled by others.").

78. Linnenbrink, *supra* at 321.

79. Slavich & Zimbardo, *supra* at 588.

80. Wolters, *supra* at 199.

81. The Telegraph, *You can do it! Scientists find urging yourself on in the second person is the key to sporting success*, https://www.telegraph.co.uk/ science/2019/07/09/can-do-scientists-find-urging-second-person-key-sporting-success/.

82. AMBROSE, *supra* at 89.

83. Barry J. Zimmerman, *Becoming a Self-Regulated Learner: An Overview*, 41 THEORY INTO PRACTICE 64, 68-69 (2002).

84. Wolters, *supra* at 194.

85. *Id.*

86. *Id.*

87. *Id.* at 195.

88. *Id.*

89. *Id.*

90. *Id.* at 196.

91. *Id.*

92. *Id.*

93. *Id.*

94. *Id.* at 199-200.

95. *Id.* at 200.

96. Adopt a growth mindset and take charge of your learning. At least that's what I think. If you disagreed with me, why did you choose something else?

Chapter Two
Change Your Study Habits

Chapter Goals.

1. To emphasize the importance of good study habits.
2. To introduce you to how the brain learns.
3. To show how this knowledge should change your study habits.
4. To introduce spaced studying.
5. To give you a study plan.
6. To stress the importance of active learning.
7. To emphasize the importance of repetition.
8. To stress the importance of self-testing (practice testing).
9. To help you understand interleaving.
10. To introduce generative learning strategies and organizational learning strategies.
11. To show what study habits are not effective.
12. To advocate for varied practice.

The most important thing you can do to improve your chances of success in law school is to adopt better study habits. As two authors have written, "The bottom line is the time spent studying does not predict academic success. The quality of the time spent studying, determined by the specific behaviors and strategies used by the learner, determines the academic success."[1]

This chapter begins by introducing you to how you learn, including the brain processes involved. The next section presents general principles of effective study. The last section gives you the details of studying, such as practice testing, spaced studying, interleaving, generative techniques, organizational learning strategies, and other learning techniques. All of the techniques in this chapter are based on the latest in general education research.[2] They are the most effective approaches for being able to remember, understand, and use knowledge.

I. An Introduction to the Brain and Learning.

Most learning does not occur in the classroom; it occurs through studying. Therefore, you need to adopt the most effective study habits.

You probably don't have effective study habits because no one ever taught you how to study. (Am I right?) You just developed study habits through trial and error, and these were probably not the most effective study habits. Poor study habits cause poor learning and understanding.

Education researchers have done a great deal of research on effective study habits in recent years. They have done this with an understanding of how the brain learns. In other words, you should base your study habits on how your brain learns.

Here is a simple explanation of how learning works:

"Brain cells [neurons] fire in patterns."[3] This process is both electrical and neurochemical.[4] Neurons pass on electrical charges to other neurons that are connected to them by synapses.[5] The firing neuron sends a chemical signal called a neurotransmitter across the synaptic gap to other neurons.[6] These signals either excite the neurons by increasing their electrical activity (causing them to fire) or inhibit their activity.[7] Neurons interact to create complex representations, concepts, and processes (chunks–interconnected neurons).[8]

"Learning is a relatively permanent change in a neuron."[9] (Reread the last sentence.) Because neurons are changed by electrical activity, "learning occurs when the firing ability of a neuron is changed."[10] Similarly, the synapses change with each firing, and linked neurons firing together strengthen the synapses.[11] Importantly for learning, "Neurons grow or die and neural connections are created or eliminated based on which ones are active."[12] In addition, practice gradually thickens the myelin coating of the axons ("long extensions connecting neurons from one area of the brain to another")[13] "improving the strength and speed of the electrical signals, and, as a result, performance."[14]

In other words, you should adopt study habits that helps your brain learn effectively: 1) strengthen neurons by firing them, 2) strengthen synapses by using them, 3) create more synapses (connections) among neurons, 4) thicken the myelin coating of axons. On the other hand, if you do not use information, the neurons and synapses will weaken or disappear. (If you don't use it; you lose it.)

Based on the above, here are five rules of learning:[15]

1. New learning requires attention.
2. Learning requires repetition.
3. Learning is about connections.

4. Some learning is effortless; some requires effort.
5. Learning is learning.

A note about no. 4, learning requires effort. Two authors have stated, "While students tend to believe that they learn the material better when the information seems clear and easy, in fact, that is not true. Students retain information longer and are able to use that information better in new situations when they work harder to learn the material."[16] Similarly, another author has written, "[H]ard learning is better learning. If the learning process is easy, the student did not really learn as much."[17]

I am sorry to be the one to tell you this, but study after study has shown that success in law school requires a great deal of effort. (Please don't shoot the messenger.) The best you can do is to adopt effective study habits so that you are putting your hard work to good use.

II. The Basics of Effective Study Habits.

Now, let's go to the big picture on study habits in connection with the above principles.

Many law students prepare for class by reading that class's cases before class, then cram for the exam using class notes and other materials a couple of days before the exam. This is not an effective learning strategy. (Isn't this how you studied in undergraduate school? Cram at the last minute? All nighters? Be honest!) Spacing studying, as opposed to massing it, helps long term-memory retention.[18] However, "spacing study feels less effective as students have to work harder to retrieve information from days or even weeks ago."[19] Students often mass learn (cram) because they think it is the best way to prepare for the exam. "Like rereading, massing study creates illusions of competence when material that is easier to recall is judged better learned than material that is harder to recall."[20] However, cramming is not the best way to retain knowledge in long-term memory, which is what the student needs to become an expert lawyer. (Remember the story of the tortoise and the hare? Who won the race? In other words, slow and steady wins the race, and this is true of studying, too. And, it's supported by actual science!)

The above is true because of how the mind works. Synapses weaken if they are unused, just like your muscles weaken if they are unused.[21] Spaced repetition helps "keep the neurons, and the synaptic signals between them, alive by repeatedly activating them."[22] "Note, however, that the learner shouldn't review the material at regular intervals. . . . It turns out that as the neurons are reactivated and the synapses again carry signals to each other, they increase their durability and need less frequent stimulation until they begin to decline again."[23]

During the semester, you should spend 1/3rd of your time preparing for class, 1/3rd of your time reflecting on what you learned in class (usually the same day as the class), and 1/3 of your time organizing and synthesizing the materials (say every weekend).[24] Preparing for class should involve more than just reading the cases so that you won't be embarrassed if called upon. You should think about the law and reasoning in the cases and how they relate to material previously learned. You should also come up with any questions you have on the material (what you didn't understand), so that you can ask questions in class. The evening after the class, you should review your class notes, rewrite them (elaboration), and self-test.[25] You should "read with the intent of re-discovering what was presented in class."[26] After you have reviewed that day's notes, you should identify the most important ideas in that class and what important procedures, such as the steps in analyzing a case, were covered. You should also question the material, asking questions such as how do these ideas relate to what we've learned before, what is the reasoning behind the rules, and are there alternatives to the law and reasoning (reflection). You should also come up with your own examples of concepts or tests. You need to synthesize (outline) the material at least once a week, using graphic organizers. (see below) This helps learning through repetition and restating the material. Outlining is not busy work. As two authors have written, "High-performing students engaged in a multistep process that included 'distilling or condensing' when outlining and consistently engaged in self-testing in the outlining process, whereas underperforming students did not outline or did not further distill their outlines."[27] Finally, you will want to study before the exam, but the above helps eliminate the need for cram-ming. Also, based on spacing and interleaving principles (see below), students should study for a particular exam over several days. (Monday-Thursday torts in the morning, contracts in the afternoon, property in the evening).

Here are two general principles of learning:

First, active learning is the most effective technique to help you learn, retain material, and use that material. As Peter Brown and his colleagues averred in the best-selling book *Make it Stick* (2014), "It is better to solve a problem than memorize a solution."[28] Similarly, active learning "is the best

26

way to teach all material in law schools, including doctrine. To have a deep understanding of the law, students must be able to use the law to craft legal arguments, draft legal documents, and shape legal strategy."[29] "Information gets into our long-term memory only if we spend time thinking about and processing the information."[30] (Got it. Be an active learner.)

It is important that you understand that learning is not a passive activity; it is one in which you must participate. (Did you learn sports by reading a book?) Memorization by itself is superficial learning; you must use the knowledge to truly learn. Active learning strategies also help you absorb complex material better than passive ones because active learning involves the brain in manipulating and processing information.[31] In other words, active learning creates new neurons, strengthens existing ones, and creates more synapses among neurons. You actually grow your brain! (Again, this has been established by actual science.)

You should also use study strategies that reinforce long-term memory[32] and create connections among concepts, processes, declarative knowledge, etc. One way of doing this is through repetition, which aids long-term memory retention because repetitions strengthen neurons.[33] Researchers have demonstrated that "average people can achieve extraordinary memory ability by developing their own retrieval structures or being given them by researchers."[34] Experts recommend at least four repetitions of material each at least once within a day for retention.[35]

III. The Details of Studying.

Here are some detailed learning techniques:

Practice testing, "[s]elf-testing or taking practice tests over to-be-learned material," is probably the most effective learning technique.[36] For one thing, "The retrieval process creates learning while gauging learning depth."[37] Several hundred studies (wow that's a lot) have demonstrated that self-testing (a type of retrieval) improves learning and retention because testing solidifies learning.[38] From a neurobiology of learning viewpoint, self-testing improves retention because it triggers elaborative retrieval processes (It is an effortful type of active learning.).[39] "Attempting to retrieve target information involves a search of long-term memory that activates related information, and this ac-tivated information may then be encoded along with the retrieved target, forming an elaborated trace that affords multiple pathways to facilitate later access to that information."[40] In other words, it causes neurons to fire strongly and strengthens synapses (connections). Moreover, practice testing also helps retention and test performance by helping students organize knowledge and process distinct features of things. In sum, you should self-test frequently while studying.

For example, you can test your knowledge of the elements of intentional torts. Memorize the elements of intentional torts, then see if you can name them. If you can't, re-memorize the elements. Then, see if you can name them. Then, wait an hour, and repeat the test. Repeat the test the next day to see if you can still remember the elements. Don't worry if self-testing is difficult at first. In fact, "The harder it is for you to recall new learning from memory, the greater the benefit of doing so."[41] (Reread this last sentence. I think it is really important. When I struggle to remember something, then it suddenly pops into my head, I always remember it the next time. The effort strengthens the neurons.) After you have memorized the intentional torts, move on to the elements of each tort, and self-test yourself on the elements. (I hope you see that this process is cumulative–you keep adding details to your knowledge.)

Above, I recommended spaced studying as a big picture technique. Specifically, with spaced studying, you spread learning of a particular item over time.[42] Spacing learning aids retention much more than massing learning (cramming).[43] When students try to cram learning into a short time, retention suffers because such learning does not involve retrieval and is too easy.[44] Moreover, "embedding new learning in long-term memory requires a process of consolidation, in which memory traces (the brain's representations of the new learning) are strengthened, given meaning, and connected to prior knowledge–a process that unfolds over hours and may take several days."[45]

Similarly, researchers have found that interleaving, which involves covering different material or doing different types of learning in the same session, is very effect for learning.[46] It is effective because it "creates space between retrieval attempts by mixing up the subjects, putting more time between testing attempts, forcing learners to distinguish between subjects, and creating deeper understanding with material."[47] For example, you could study torts, then property, then come back to torts. Interleaving is effective because it is difficult; it requires effortful learning.[48] In addition, it helps you develop your problem-solving skills because you can compare different solutions to problems in different fields.[49] In other words, interleaved learning helps you develop the ability to use knowledge and skills in new contexts, which is called domain transfer (see Chapter Five).[50] Interleaving also requires you to retrieve information from long-term memory, thus enhancing long-term memory.[51]

Generative techniques are also very effective for learning because they involve active learning. Rewriting your class notes is a simple example of a generative technique.[52] This helps you remember and understand the information your professor wants you to learn.

Elaborative interrogation is "[g]enerating an explanation for why an explicitly stated fact or concept is true."[53] This technique is effective because it causes the learner to draw on prior knowledge to generate an explanation for a fact or concept.[54] This activates pre-existing schema (organized material) in the mind, which helps organize the new information by processing similarities and differences between the new and old material.[55] Relating new information to prior knowledge strengthens the retention of the new information and creates more connections among items stored in long-term memory, which helps retention and retrieval.[56] (Did you notice that I underlined the previous sentence? It probably means it is important.)

Self-explanation, another generative technique, is "[e]xplaining how new information is related to known information, or explaining steps taken during problem solving."[57] Self-explanation requires you to explain your learning process.[58] It improves learning by relating new learning to old learning.[59] In other words, it creates new connections among neurons.

An advanced example of the generative effect is synthesis of multiple sources. Synthesis is one of the best tools to help you learn because it requires you to transform or process knowledge into something new. "In particular, students may benefit conceptually from learning tasks that promote the construction of a situation model, whereas tasks that can be performed with a more superficial representation of the text, such as using a textbase, [such as taking notes from a single treatise] would not lead to better understanding. This distinction is consistent with the idea that the construction of mental models is the key to students' deeper understanding of subject matter."[60] In addition, "in order for students to gain a deeper understanding of the subject matter, writing tasks must require knowledge-transforming and not just knowledge-telling [the passive transfer of information from text to paper]." One way to do this is to access a variety of sources, and construct your own analysis on the information you have read.[61] An example of synthesis is writing a short essay on a subject, such as defamation, using a variety of sources (say, two encyclopedias and two treatises) for a particular purpose. Of course, a common example of synthesis in legal analysis is synthesizing cases, which I will discuss in depth in a later chapter.[62]

Organizational learning strategies (which are also generative strategies), such as outlining, integrating, and synthesizing, engenders more learning than passive strategies, such as rereading or rote learning, because active engagement produces more learning than passive strategies.[63] (Didn't I say this earlier?) Most importantly, "[o]rganizing requires students to understand how individual components relate to each other to form a coherent whole."[64] You can organize information into a graphic organizer–"a type of organizing strategy such as a hierarchy chart, a flowchart, or a mindmap."[65] Visual aids are an excellent method of helping create schemas in long-term memory.[66] Using graphic organizers at the end of a unit (such as intentional torts) reinforces long-term memory and creates connections among concepts (schemas).[67] For example, you could make a poster that teaches others the fundamentals of a unit, such as making a poster teaching adverse possession. You can also use charts to help synthesize cases. Finally, it is important to note that "the processes of synthesizing cases and creating an outline helps the student store her understanding of the rule of law in long-term memory more effectively than reading a commercial outline."[68] There are no short cuts to expert learning.

Many legal education reformers suggest that students keep a journal concerning their experiences in class.[69] "This activity . . . requires students to write down their reflections on the learning contents from a previous lesson," highlighting the main ideas, generating examples, and noting comprehension problems.[70] The journal should also contain your graphic organizers.

As I mentioned above, when studying, you should relate new material to material studied before, which creates connections with the previous knowledge and allows more ways to retrieve the material from long-term memory.[71] Does the new material add to, reinforce, or contradict the old material? Does the new material help me understand the old material better?

You may want to add the above techniques to your learning repertoire slowly. I would suggest you start with spaced studying and self-testing, then add the others one-by-one.

Researchers have demonstrated that several common study techniques are ineffective, including summarization, highlighting, the keyword mnemonic, imagery use for text learning, and just rereading.[72] (How many of these did you use in college?) These techniques are ineffective because they are too easy; they don't require your brain to work. As two authors have stated, "Rereading tricks us into thinking we learn more than we actually do."[73]

If you don't believe me, listen to a learning expert: "Re-reading and highlighting are particularly ineffective. They're just passive, and you are just kind of skimming that material. It makes you feel better. You feel comfortable with the material, but you don't really know the material. Doing things that are a little bit more difficult, that require you to really make connections, is a better way to learn. [You might] explain things to yourself, [or] simply quiz yourself."[74] (I know that it is hard to break old habits, but you have to discard these ones if you want to do well in law school.)

In sum, the more different approaches you use studying the better because it creates more connections (multimodal learning).[75] Varied practice, learning knowledge or a skill in different ways, helps transfer learning from one context to another because different types of learning use different parts of the brain.[76] You could first read the cases before class using the reading skills from Chapter Three. You would then participate in class, taking notes. (See Chapter Six) That evening, you should review your notes and write about that day's class in your journal. You could also test your recall of the day's material to aid retrieval. You should also reflect on what you learned that day. The next weekend you could organize that day's ideas with the rest of the unit in a graphic organizer such as an outline. You could also read in a hornbook about that unit. In subsequent weekends, you could also review your graphic organizers for the whole semester and further test your recall. Finally, you could prepare for the test by studying your notes, testing your recall, and reviewing your graphic organizers.

Sounds hard? Yes, it does, but if you use these techniques you will do much better in law school than those who kept their ineffective study methods from college.

Summary
Learning Techniques that are Effective

1. Active learning
2. Repetition
3. Self-testing
4. Spaced-studying
5. Interleaving
6. Elaborative interrogation
7. Self-explanation
8. Synthesis of multiple sources
9. Outlining
10. Graphic organizers
11. Journaling

12. Relating new material to prior knowledge
13. Multimodal learning

Learning Techniques that are Ineffective

1. Just re-reading
2. Highlighting
3. The keyword mnemonic
4. Passive learning techniques

Exercises

1. Why does most learning occur outside the classroom?
2. Think about the study habits you used in college? Based on this chapter, do you think they were effective or not? Do you understand why?
3. How does learning work based on cognitive psychology?
4. Can you see why it is important to understand how learning works?
5. What are the five rules of learning?
6. What is attention? Does the human brain have limited or broad attention? What does this mean for studying? (I'm going to give you the answer to this one. Just study. No cell phones, no tv, etc.)
7. What does "learning is about connections" mean?
8. Why does learning require effort?
9. What does "learning is learning" mean?
10. What is spaced studying? Why is it more effective than cramming? How much do students retain with cramming?
11. Why is active learning more effective than passive learning?
12. Write down all the effective study techniques you can remember? Are these active or passive approaches?
13. Why is repetition important? What is the best way to do repetition?
14. What is practice testing? Why is it so effective? Did you use it in college? Do you think you would have gotten better grades if you had used self-testing? Can you see how you should use it in law school?
15. What is spaced studying? Why is it so effective? Did you use spaced studying in college?
16. What is interleaving? Why is it effective?
17. Name and explain several generative learning techniques? Why are they effective?
18. What are organizational learning strategies? How do they help you learn?

19. Have you ever used graphic organizers? Do you see how they can help you organize material and retain that material in your long-term memory?

20. Do you see why commercial outlines or canned briefs can hurt your learning? (I'm going to answer this one, too. They hurt your learning because they do an important part of the learning for you. In other words, when you use commercial outlines and canned briefs, you miss learning legal reasoning techniques that you need to succeed on exams. You can use them to double-check your outline, but never use a commercial outline instead of doing the work yourself.)

21. What study techniques are ineffective? Why? Did you use these techniques in college? Can you have gotten better grades in college if you had used different techniques?

22. Why is using a variety of study techniques important?

23. Write out a plan on how you will study in law school.

Finally, you need to make sure you are using the proper learning techniques for the type of class. For example, law students often are studying the wrong things when they study for doctrinal classes. Students generally try to memorize material so that they can do well on the exam (get a good grade). However, doing well on exams also involves the ability to apply what the students have learned to a factual situation. Thus, students also need to study reasoning, analytical, and problem-solving skills when studying for doctrinal courses. One way to do this is to take practice exams.[77]

Exercise

1. Write down the five most important things you learned from this chapter.

Notes

1. Jennifer M. Cooper & Regan A. R. Gurung, *Smarter Law Study Habits: An Empirical Analysis of Learning Strategies and Relationship with Law GPA*, 62 ST. LOUIS U. L.J. 361, 367-8 (2018).

2. There have been hundred of studies on the effectiveness of good study habits. JOHN A. C. HATTIE, VISIBLE LEARNING: A SYNTHESIS OF OVER 800 META-ANALYSES RELATING TO ACHIEVEMENT 22 (2009).

3. PAUL THAGARD, THE BRAIN AND THE MEANING OF LIFE 44 (2010) (quoting Steven Pinker). *See also* DUANE F. SHELL ET.AL., THE UNIFIED LEARNING MODEL: HOW MOTIVATIONAL, COGNITIVE, AND NEURO-BIOLOGICAL SCIENCES INFORM BEST TEACHING PRACTICES 8-9 (2010). Neurons are the "atoms"of the brain–the building blocks of the brain. You can also compare them to the bits in computer memory. Humans are born with approximately 100 billion neurons. PETER C. BROWN ET.AL., MAKE IT STICK: THE SCIENCE OF SUCCESSFUL LEARNING 166 (2014). "Neurons are shaped like trees with information receiving dendrite branches and long axon trunks." Debra S. Austin, *Windmills of Your Mind: Understanding the Neurobilogy of Emotion*, https://papers.ssrn.com/sol3/papers.cfm?abstract_id=3374006 (2019). Benedict Carey has aptly called a neuron a "biological switch." BENEDICT CAREY, HOW WE LEARN: THE SURPRISING TRUTH ABOUT WHEN, WHERE, AND WHY IT HAPPENS 6 (2014). He continued, "It receives signals from one side and–when it "flips" or fires–sends a signal out the other, to the neurons to which it's linked." *Id.*

4. "Neurotransmitters are released from the presynaptic neuron where they travel to the receptors on the postsynaptic neuron, and the chemical information becomes electrical again once the chemical has docked in the receptor of the second neuron." Austin, *supra*.

5. THAGARD, *supra* at 44. I will use synapse when I am referring to the connections between neurons. I will use connections in its more general meaning.

6. *Id.* at 44-45.

7. *Id.* at 45.

8. *Id.* at 46-50; Duane F. SHELL ET.AL., THE UNIFIED LEARNING MODEL: HOW MOTIVATIONAL, COGNITIVE, AND NEUROLOGICAL SCIENCES INFORM BEST TEACHING PRACTICES 12 (2010).

9. SHELL, *supra* at 7.
    Professor Pinker points out that "the brain changes when we learn." STEVEN PINKER, THE BLANK SLATE: THE MODERN DENIAL OF HUMAN NATURE 85 (2002).

10. SHELL, *supra* at 8.

11. *Id.* at 9.

12. *Id.*

13. Susan Stuart & Ruth Vance, *Bringing a Knife to the Gunfight: The Academically Unprepared Law Students and Legal Education Reform*, 48 Val. L. Rev. 41, 76 (2013).

14. BROWN, *supra* at 170-171.

15. SHELL, *supra* at 14-15.

16. Karen McDonald Henning & Julia Belian, *If You Give a Mouse a Cookie: Increasing Assessments and Individual Feedback in Law School Classes*, 95 U. DET. MERCY L. REV. 35, 48 (2018).

17. Louis N. Schulze, *Using Science to Build Better Learners: One School's Successful Efforts to Raise Its Bar Passage Rates in an Era of Decline*, 28 https://papers.ssrn.com/sol3/papers.cfm?abstract_id=2960192 ("[H]ard learning is better learning. If the learning process is easy, the student did not really learn as much."); *see also* BROWN, *supra* at 3 ("Learning is deeper and more durable when it is *effortful*.").

18. Jessica M. Logan et.al., *Metacognition and the Spacing Effect: the Role of Repetition, Feedback, and In-struction on Judgments of Learning for Massed and Spaced Rehearsal*, 7 Metacognition Learning 175, 176 (2012). [http://castel.psych.ucla.edu/papers/Logan%20JOL%20Spacing%20ML.pdf].

19. Cooper & Gurung, *supra* at 372.

20. *Id.*

21. Schulze, *supra* at 15.

22. *Id.*

23. *Id.*

24. For a similar strategy, see Carol Andrews, *Four Simple Lessons about the Needs of First-Year Law Students*, 18/2 THE LAW TEACHER 4, 4-5 (2012).

25. Professor Schwartz notes, "[i]f students can accurately restate a rule in their own words, they understand it." Michael Hunter Schwartz, *Improving Legal Education by Improving Casebooks: Fourteen Things Casebooks Can Do to Produce Better and More Learning*, 3 ELON L. REV. 27, 41 (2011) [hereinafter Schwartz, *Casebooks*].

26. Leamnson, *supra* at 8.

27. Cooper & Gurung, *supra* at 375.

28. BROWN, *supra*.

29. Jessica Erickson, *Experiential Education in the Lecture Hall*, 6 N.E.L.J. 87, 8 (2013).

30. *Id.* at 91.

31. Robin A. Boyle, *Employing Active-Learning Techniques and Metacognition in Law School: Shifting Energy from Professor to Student*, 81 U. DET.-MERCY L. REV. 1, 3-4 (2003); Paula Lustbader, From Dreams to Reality: The Emerging Role of Law School Academic Support

Programs, 31 U.S.F. L. REV. 839, 855 (1997); *see also* Gerald F. Hess, *Heads and Hearts: The Teaching and Learning Environment in Law School*, 52 J. LEGAL EDUC. 75, 102 (2002) ("Active learning methods are effective in achieving many of the primary goals of legal education, including higher-level thinking skills (analysis, synthesis, evaluation, and critical thinking), content mastery (By developing knowledge and concepts, students attain a deeper level of understanding), professional skills . . . and positive attitude . . .").

32. "Memory traces are fragile and at risk of becoming extinct." Austin, *supra.*

33. SHELL, *supra* at 8-9 ("The more the neuron fires, the easier it is to fire again."), 24-25. Repetition is much more than rote memorization or "drill and kill." *Id.* at 181. Repetition is most effective when there is variety in the repetition. Contextualizing also gives variety to repetition. *Id.*

34. CAROL S. DWECK, MINDSET: THE NEW PSYCHOLOGY OF SUCCESS 16 (2006).

35. SHELL, *supra* at 24-25.

36. John Dunlosky et.al., *Improving Students' Learning With Effective Learning Techniques: Promising Directions From Cognitive and Edu-cational Psychology*, 14 Psychological Science in the Public Interest 6 (2013) [http://marker.to/XVMEI9]. *See also* Louis N. Schulze, *Using Science to Build Better Learners: One School's Successful Efforts to Raise Its Bar Passage Rates in an Era of Decline*, https://papers.ssrn.com/sol3/papers.cfm?abstract_id=2960192 at 4.

37. Cooper & Gurung, *supra* at 370.

38. Dunlosky, *supra* at 29; BROWN, *supra* at 28-39. In one study of the testing effect, students scored a grade level higher on material that had been quizzed in comparison to material that had not been quizzed. BROWN, *supra* at 35.

39. Dunlosky, *supra* at 30.

40. *Id.*

41. BROWN ET.AL., *supra* at 202. These authors noted, "[p]eople commonly believe that if you expose yourself to something enough times–say, a textbook passage or a set of terms from an eighth grade biology class, you can burn them into memory. Not so." *Id.* at 9.

42. Dunlosky, *supra* at 6.

43. *Id.* at 35; Henry L. Roediger III & Mary A. Pyc, *Inexpensive Techniques to Improve Education: Applying Cognitive Psychology to Enhance Educational Practice*, 1 J. APPLIED RESEARCH IN MEMORY AND COGNITION 242, 24243 (2012) [http://www.bryanburnham.net/ wp-content/uploads/.014/01/Roediger-Pyc-2012-Inexpensive-techniques-to-improve-educati on-Applying-cognitive-psychology-to-enhance-educational-practice.pdf] ("If information is repeated in a distributed fashion or spaced over time, it is learned more slowly but is retained for

much longer."). Psychologist William James explained why cramming is ineffective: "Things learned in a few hours, on one occasion, for one purpose, cannot possibly have formed many associations with other things in the mind. Their brain-processes are led into by few paths, and are relatively little liable to be awakened again. Speedy oblivion is the almost inevitable fate of all that is committed to memory in this simple way." WILLIAM JAMES, THE PRINCIPLES OF PSYCHOLOGY 445 (1890). The only thing that one can add today to James's explanation is that the "associations" are neural connections–synapses.

44. Dunlosky, *supra* at 36. Spaced practice involves "effortful recall of learning." BROWN, *supra* at 82.

45. BROWN, *supra* at 49.

46. Dunlosky, *supra* at 6; *see also* BROWN, *supra* at 49-50.

47. Cooper & Gurung, *supra* at 373.

48. BROWN, *supra* at 85.

49. Dunlosky, *supra* at 40, 41.

50. Roediger & Pyc, *supra* at 243-44.

51. Dunlosky, *supra* at 41.

52. I don't mean just recopying your notes. In rewriting them, reorganize them, stress the important material, and omit irrelevant material.

53. Dunlosky, *supra* at 6; *see also* DANIEL T. WILLINGHAM, WHY DON'T STUDENTS LIKE SCHOOL? 63 (2009).

54. Dunlosky, *supra* at 8. "For example, if they learn that it takes Neptune longer than Mars to revolve around the sun, they should ask themselves why this is the case. By trying to answer the 'why' question, the students have to think the issue through to understand it and then they will remember it better." Roediger & Pyc, *supra* at 246.

55. Dunlosky, *supra* at 8.

56. BROWN, *supra* at 5; see also MARYBETH HERALD, YOUR BRAIN AND LAW SCHOOL: A CONTEXT AND PRACTICE BOOK 51 (2014).

57. Dunlosky, *supra* at 6. "For example, while reading a new page of text, they might be asking themselves: What facts on this page do I already know? What facts are new?" Roediger & Pyc, *supra* at 246.

58. Dunlosky, *supra* at 11.

59. *Id.* at 11; SUSAN A. AMBROSE ET.AL., HOW LEARNING WORKS: 7 RESEARCH-BASED PRINCIPLES FOR SMART TEACHING 15 (Jossey Bass 2010) ("In essence, new knowledge "sticks" better when it has prior knowledge to stick to.").

60. Jennifer Wiley & James F. Voss, *Constructing Arguments from Multiple Sources: Tasks that Promoting Understanding and Not Just Memory for Text*, 91 J. EDUC. PSYCH. 301, 301 (1999).

61. *Id.* at 309.

62. Synthesizing the law is a vital skill for law students. Not only is it the way to determine what the law is, synthesizing the law helps law students develop important learning skills. Professor Burgess has remarked, when students synthesize cases, "[s]tudents are not 'creating law'; rather they are creating *their own understanding* of how the cases work together. . . . The understanding of the law that they create must match the understanding of the law that the profession (or at least their professor) generally accepts as accurate." Hillary Burgess, *Deepening the Discourse Using The Legal Mind's Eye: Lessons from Neuroscience and Psychology that Optimize Law School Learning*, 29 QUINNIPIAC L. REV. 1, 20 (2011).

63. Michael Hunter Schwartz, *Teaching Law by Design: How Learning Theory and Instructional Design Can Inform and Reform Law Teaching*, 38 SAN DIEGO L. REV. 347, 375 (2001) [hereinafter Schwartz, *Law Teaching*].

64. Burgess, *supra* at 17.

65. Schwartz, *Casebooks*, *supra* at 46. For various examples of graphic organizers, see Burgess, *supra* at 58-74 and MICHAEL HUNTER SCHWARTZ & DENISE RIEBE, CONTRACTS: A CONTEXT AND PRACTICE CASEBOOK 71-80 (2009).

66. Burgess, *supra* at 41.

67. *See Id.* at 33 ("Graphical organizers also help novices create efficient organizational systems for their knowledge and weed out inefficient or incorrect connections.").

68. *Id.* at 37.

69. ROBERT J. MARZANO ET.AL, BECOMING A REFLECTIVE TEACHER 10 (2012). MARZANO, *supra* at 10; *see generally* Julian Roelle et.al., *The Use of Solved Example Problems for Fostering Strategies of Self-Regulated Learning in Journal Writing*, 2012 Education Research International 1. [http://downloads.hindawi.com/journals/edu/2012/751625.pdf].

70. Roelle, *supra* at 2.

71. Tonya Kowalski, *True North: Transfer for the Navigation of Learning in Legal Education*, 2010 SEATTLE U. L. REV. 51, 73.

72. Dunlosky, *supra* at 5. As one scholar has stated, "not just any repetition will do." WIL-LINGHAM, *supra* at 59; *see also* Cooper & Gurung, *supra* at 389-0 (study of law students at two law schools).

73. Cooper & Gurung, *supra* at 369-70.

74. Olga Khazan, *How to Learn New Things as an Adult (An Interview with Ulrich Boser)*, [https://www.theatlantic.com/science/archive/2017/03/how-to-learn-new-things-as-an-adult/519687/)

75. Burgess, *supra* at 45-47.

76. BROWN, *supra* at 51.

77. Most law schools keep practice exams on-line or in the library.

Chapter Three
How to Read and Brief A Case

Chapter Goals.

1. To teach you how to read texts effectively.
2. To explain the importance of active reading.
3. To teach you about the three stages of reading: pre-reading, reading, and the reflective stage.
4. To teach you how to read and analyze (brief) cases.
5. To demonstrate the dangers of using canned briefs.
6. To give you an example of a case analysis (brief).
7. To introduce you to the five types of legal reasoning, and to show you how to identify them in cases.

Reading and briefing cases is one of the most important things you will do in law school. I will discuss reading and briefing cases in the second half of this chapter, but, first, I need to help you improve your reading ability–your ability to fully understand complicated texts.

I. How to Read Difficult Texts.

I hate to be the one to break this to you, but you probably aren't reading texts effectively. I mean you aren't getting everything out of the text you can.

I know you learned how to read in the first grade. Considering that you are on the verge of law school, you probably learned how to read sooner than most of your classmates. But, did anyone ever teach you advanced reading skills–how to fully comprehend a text? I'm guessing no, based on my fifteen years of teaching law students.

Effective reading skills are vital for law school success. Law school requires a great deal of reading, and you are expected to fully understand and remember what you have read.

Here is what you need to be a better reader:

First, reading is not a passive skill; it is an active one. You need to be an engaged reader. You need to interact with the text, talk back to the text, and reflect on the text.

Second, reading is not a race. It is not important how quickly you read a text, but how much you understand. Forget anything you have ever heard about speed reading. You can't properly comprehend a text while you are reading it fast. Can you properly view scenery while driving down the highway at 80 mph?

Finally and most importantly, <u>reading is thinking</u>. In law school, you are learning to think like a lawyer. Reading texts, cases, statutes, and other materials, is an important part of learning to think like a lawyer.

Reading is a process, so let's divide it into three stages: 1) pre-reading, 2) reading, and 3) reflection.[1] Each of these stages are equally important for effective reading.

A. Pre-Reading

Do you have a <u>pre-reading</u> routine? Probably not. In fact, you are probably asking what I am talking about. You just read. However, pre-reading is necessary to fully comprehend a text. Pre-reading can be divided into several substages.

With pre-reading, you prepare yourself to read; you get ready for the text. (When you play basketball, don't you warm up first? Doesn't the coach tell you want to do in the game?)

First, you should <u>understand what the reading is</u>. A case? A statute? An encyclopedia? A comic book? Each type of text requires a different approach to reading that text. (You wouldn't practice your tennis swing to get ready for football season, would you?)

Next, <u>ask yourself your purpose in reading the text</u>. Remember, in Chapter One, I said that having a purpose with a task helps motivate you for that task. Also, having a purpose will help you decide how you will approach the text. For example, you are reading a case on personal jurisdiction for your summer job so that you can write an analysis of whether a jurisdiction has personal jurisdiction over your client. (Isn't having a purpose also important in sports?) Remember that having a learning goal, rather than a performance goal, leads to better learning.

Next, <u>put the reading into context</u>. First, answer the simple questions. With a case, know the parties, the date of the opinion, the level of the court, the procedure below (if any), and the jurisdiction. Second, what narrative does the reading fit into? For example, a personal jurisdiction case would fit into the narrative of Supreme Court cases on personal jurisdiction under the due process clause. Finally, ask how the reading fits into your prior knowledge. If you lack prior knowledge for a reading you may want to do some background reading in a secondary source. For example, if you know nothing about personal jurisdiction, you might read about personal jurisdiction in a treatise or legal encyclopedia. (In sports, don't you relate a new skill to a known one?)

In the second pre-reading substage, the reader "assesses her efficacy for accomplishing the task."[2] (Remember that I discussed self-efficacy in the first chapter, and it is as important to reading as it is to motivation.) In other words, am I capable of doing the reading? You should know your skill and experience levels, and you should believe you can improve those levels. As I mentioned in Chapter One, students who have positive attitudes and confidence in themselves learn more. (Don't you need self-efficacy in sports? Don't athletes go into slumps when they lose confidence?)

Self-motivation is also important in the pre-reading stage. Someone who wants to read a text is more motivated than someone who has to read something. Remember how I stressed the importance of learning goals in Chapter One. This is especially important in law school where you can go on autopilot because of all the reading. One way to help self-motivation is replacing negative self-talk (usually from prior learning experiences) with positive self-talk a(from positive prior experiences) and a sense of self as an effective learner (self-efficacy). (Could athletes make it through long practices without self-motivation?) (Remember, self-talk should be in the second person.)

In the final pre-reading substage, you should develop a reading strategy (how you will approach the reading) based on the earlier substages.[3] "Reading strategies are 'set[s] of mental processes used by a reader to achieve a purpose.'"[4] You should think about the steps you will take in reading the case, and the tools you will use. For a beginning legal reader, it might help to write down your reading strategy. Of course, a large part of a strategy for reading cases is to incorporate the case analysis techniques set forth in the following section. (Don't batters have a strategy when they face a pitcher? "I will look for fastballs because this guy can't get his slider over the plate.")

I bet you are thinking that the pre-reading stage adds a lot of work to your reading. It doesn't, at least, in the long run. If you practice pre-reading for a while, it will become almost automatic, and it will not take up much of your time. On the other hand, adding pre-reading to your reading routine will focus you, thus helping comprehension, and it will save time in the long run because your reading will be more efficient.

B. The Performance (Reading) Stage

Now you do the actual reading. This stage encompasses three sub-stages: (1) "attention-focusing," (2) "the activity itself," and (3) "the self-monitoring."[5] (You didn't think it was going to be simple did you?) Attention-focusing helps make the reading productive. Efficient readers are able to focus their attention.[6] Having a strategy, purpose, and goal when reading helps attention-focusing. (Now you know why the pre-reading stage is important.) Moreover, avoid multi-tasking while you are reading because it hurts the attention you can give to the reading. This just isn't my idea, a group of neuroscientists have declared, ""Multitasking violates everything scientists know about memory formation.""[7] (Isn't attention-focusing also important for athletes? Do baseball players check their cellphones after every pitch? Why not?)

In the activity substage, you should be an active reader. You must work to understand the text; the text itself is passive. You won't remember anything if you just passively read the text.

You should first skim the case to obtain a general sense of what it is about (including deciding what is important and what is irrelevant), then you should read the text carefully. (When skimming focus on headings and the topic sentences of paragraphs.) You should use the tools of critical thinking: "interpretation, analysis, evaluation, inference, explanation, and self-regulation."[8] You should read and understand every word and how words, sentences, and paragraphs fit together. (Re-read the previous sentence before going on.) You should be prepared to shift between larger and smaller concepts to check the consistency of the big picture you are creating.[9] Finally, "Because of its ambiguity, [reading] needs a lot of inference-making, interpretation and reading between the lines."[10]

Self-monitoring is also an important part of reading. Self-monitoring (using your inner voice) is simultaneous with the activity stage. First, you should consider how well you are thinking about the material (internal feedback).[11] How well are you understanding it? Being a recursive reader is an important part of self-monitoring. If you don't understand something, read a passage again or go back to an earlier passage. Persistence is a characteristic of self-regulated readers;[12] they don't let obstacles stop them. You should also always look up words you do not understand.

You should evaluate the text as you are reading it (engage the text and use your inner critic). You should think about the structure of the text.[13] How is it organized? Why is it organized this way? You should talk back to the text.[14] You should question and criticize the text. Write down your questions and comments. If you mark a passage in the text, make sure you know why you marked that passage. Connect the case with prior knowledge. (This last technique is very important because it helps you put a reading in context, and it helps you organize the subject.)

(Self-monitoring is key for athletes. A batter self-monitors as he faces the pitcher. The batter tries to determine what the pitcher is doing, so that the hitter can get a hit on the next swing. The batter also self-monitors what he is doing. "You swung at a bad pitch. Don't do it again.")

C. Post-Reading (Reflective) Stage

After you finish the reading, you should reflect on the reading and evaluate how well you did on the reading. In this stage, you should critically reflect on what you've read and consider the implications of the reading, with your inner voice.[15] You should consider how the reading changed your concept of the subject.

I can't underestimate the importance of reflection. I never heard the word reflect once in law school. I doubt it is any better today. Yet reflection helps you remember material, and, more importantly, it helps make you a critical thinker. Just sit back it a chair, and think about the text. Let your critical side be free.

You should also evaluate how well you did on the reading. Did you fully understand the reading? (If not, read it again.) Did it take longer to read the case than it should have? If so, why? Did you have enough context (background) before you read the case? How did your reading strategy work? What did you get from the reading, and how does this relate to your prior knowledge? How did you feel after you read the case? Did you feel better because you learned something? Effective readers feel better about themselves because they learned something while reading and accomplished their learning goals.[16] Similarly, don't tear yourself up if you didn't understand something, didn't know something, or made a mistake. All humans make mistakes. You should admit it when you've made a mistake, but don't get overly emotional about it. Instead, think about how you can improve. You should only get mad at yourself if you haven't tried hard enough.

Concerning implications of the reading, can you improve your reading process, such as improving your reading strategy? Substantively, how did the case you read change your concept of the area of the law? How can the case apply to different sets of facts (hypothesizing)? (Don't athletes evaluate their performance so that they can do better next time?)

How to Succeed in Law School

Summary of the Effective Reading Process.

I. Pre-Reading
      A. Task perception
      B. Self-Efficacy
      C. Self-Motivation
      D. Goal setting
      E. Strategic planning

II. Reading or Performance
      A. Attention focusing
      B. The reading itself
      C. Self-monitoring

III. Reflection
      A. Reflection on the reading
      B. Reflect on your reading process

Exercises

1. After reading the above section, do you think you can improve your reading strategy?
2. What are the three stages of reading? Why are there three stages to reading?
3. Why is the pre-reading stage important?
4. When you were in college, did you think about the text before you started to read it?
5. When you read a text in college, did you first identity the purpose behind your reading? Why is identifying the purpose important? Is it better to read a text because it has been assigned to you or because you have a learning goal? (You can do both.)
6. Why is putting the reading into context important?
7. When you were in college, did you compare the reading to your prior knowledge? Why is this important?
8. Why is self-efficacy important to effective reading?
9. Why is self-motivation important to effective reading?
10. Do you have a reading strategy? Why is having a reading strategy important?
11. Think about a nonfiction text you like? Consider how you would apply

the above pre-reading substages to that reading.

12. What are the three substages of the reading stage? Why is each important?

13. What is attention focusing?

14. Do you usually do something else, like listen to music, while you are reading? How does this affect your attention focusing?

15. Why is being an active reader important?

16. What does criticize the text mean? Do you critically think about the texts you read? Why is this important?

17. What is self-monitoring? Do you monitor the effectiveness of your reading while you are reading? Why is self-monitoring important?

18. Do you try to get everything you can get out of a text, or do you just read it passively, hoping that your brain will absorb some of it? Are you a "persistent" reader?

19. Are you a recursive reader? Why is this important?

20. Do you evaluate a text while you are reading it? Why is this important?

21. Do you write down questions and comments you have about a reading?

22. What should you do in the post-reading stage? Why is this stage important?

23. Why is reflection an important part of reading? Do you generally reflect on what you've read? Can you see how reflection helps your understand a text?

24. Do you evaluate how well you have done a reading–whether you have understood the text and read it efficiently? Can you see how your reading ability will improve if you evaluate your reading effectiveness?

25. Can you see how making mistakes helps your ability to learn? Don't be afraid of making mistakes; learn from them.

26. Find a short informative reading. Apply the above process to that reading? Can you see how your reading effectiveness improves when you adopt a reading process?

The above section has shown how you can significantly improve your reading ability. You can remember more of what you have read, you can understand it better, and you can use your knowledge better. In the first chapter, I talked about the growth mindset. Can you see how improving your reading ability improves your intelligence, and supports the growth mindset?

II. Reading and Briefing Cases.

Reading and briefing cases is one of the most important things you will do in the first year of law school because it helps you develop your legal reasoning ability–how to think like a lawyer. I advise you to brief every case you read for a class during your first year. Otherwise, you will struggle in law school, and you won't do well on exams.

Some older, and supposedly wiser, students will tell you that everything I said in the above paragraph is wrong. You don't need to brief cases for very long, and there is a simple short cut–canned briefs. Canned briefs contain briefs of cases in the case books. They look very much like the briefs I will present below. In fact, there are free on-line canned briefs, but I am certainly not going to name them.

Canned briefs are bad because they do the work for you. As I discussed before, briefing cases develops your legal reasoning ability, and you need to practice this skill again and again and again. If you take a short cut by using canned briefs, you will lose a vital part of your legal education. You will struggle throughout law school, you will get low grades, and you will struggle to get a well-paying job. You might as well take poison.

How do I know this. First, I graduated second in my law school class, and I briefed cases for the entire first year. I never bought canned briefs. Second, I have observed which students did well and which students did poorly for fifteen years of teaching. I knew who was reading canned briefs and who wasn't.

Finally, the purpose of reading and briefing cases in law school is to understand and remember what is in the cases. It is not to get through the assignment as quickly as possible.

Lawyers read cases differently than they read most texts. First, let's understand what cases are. They are opinions on the law. They are not scripture written on the sky. They are not the objective truth. Yes, they are the law in the sense that they are authority, but they are actually interpretations of the law, and interpretations can change. Great minds can differ. For example, many cases include multiple opinions, including dissents, which disagree withe the majority opinion. A dissent is not necessarily wrong; it just didn't get enough votes to prevail. In sum, let's start with the idea that cases are one judge's or a group of judges' opinions on what the law is.

The meaning of written cases is also open to interpretation. Different lawyers can get different (reasonable) meanings out of the same case. When you analyze cases to give your client an opinion of what the law is, you are trying to come up with the reasonable objective interpretation of the case–the one a court is most likely to apply. However, when you are arguing your client's case to the court, you give the case the best reasonable interpretation that will help your client.[17] (Do you see the difference? If not, reflect on this.) In sum, when you read cases you are giving meaning to the case based on your purpose in reading it.

While reading cases, you should use all the techniques I talked about in the first part of this chapter. The pre-reading stage is especially important for reading cases. In particular, make sure you have a purpose for the reading and that you relate the case you are reading to cases you have read before on the same subject. As mentioned above, as far as purpose is concerned, think about why you are reading the case. "I am reading this case to give my client an objective opinion of what the law is." "I am reading this case to give my client the possible interpretations of the law." "I am reading this case to argue for my client in a brief."

For the reading stage, devote all your attention to the reading. You can't read a case and do something else at the same time, such as watch tv. Reading cases will be very hard at the beginning, and you need to devote your attention to the reading task. (Note: Reading cases will get easier after a few weeks, especially if you follow the advice in this chapter.) Be an active reader. Treat the text critically. Talk back to the case. Question the case. Compare the case to similar cases. Come up with alternatives to what the case says. Cases often include dissents and concurrences. You need to read these dissents and concurrences because they present alternate ways of looking at the same facts and law by fined-tuned legal minds.) Self-monitor your reading of the case. Do you fully understand the case? If not, read more slowly or re-read a passage you are having trouble with.

Finally, sit back for a few minutes, and think about the case. Can you discuss the case in your own words? Reflect. (Why do I keep underlining this word?) How does this case relate to prior cases? How has the case changed the existing law? What are the case's implications for future cases? Why did the judge rule the way she did (reasoning)? Is the judge's reasoning correct? Can you produce a dissent or concurrence? Finally, evaluate how you have performed the reading task. Did you read the case correctly? Did you fully understand the case? Did you get everything out of the case that was there? Did you read the cases efficiently?

Let's talk about the details of briefing cases. Actually, I prefer "case analysis" to briefing cases. This is because analysis means to break something into parts to see how it works. When you dissected a frog in high school biology, you cut it into parts to see how the frog functioned. When analyzing a case, you break it into parts to see how it works and to understand it better. Briefing cases is active learning just like dissecting frogs is active learning.

There are four main parts to a case brief:

The Issue
The Facts
The Holding
The Reasoning

<u>Issue</u>: <u>The issue is the question that the judge is supposed to answer</u>. Answering the issue determines the case's outcome. A case can have more than one issue; several issues can determine the outcome of the case.

An issue is usually a combination of the law and the facts. It is generally very specific based on the case's facts so that the court's attention can focus specifically on what is in controversy.

Examples.
1. Does the fact that Jones was secretly drunk when he entered into the oral contract with Smith negate his acceptance of the contract, meaning that no contract was formed?
2. Was Jones's failure to stop at the stop light the cause of the accident?
3. Did the landlord breach the lease with the tenant when he failed to provide electricity and heat to tenant's apartment for 24 hours during a cold streak, when the failure was due to bad weather that prevented him from getting necessary parts?

Notice how specific I framed the issues, especially the last one. Can you see what I gave you for no. 3 is better than writing "did the landlord breach the lease"? Being specific focuses your learning.

<u>Facts</u>: <u>The material facts are those facts that determine the outcome</u>. You should leave out all irrelevant facts, although you can include background facts to help you understand the context. You should start your facts with a strong topic sentence. Organize the facts in a coherent order. Note that the court may not have written the facts in a comprehensible structure. In that case, you need to rewrite the facts so that you can clearly understand them.

You should also include the procedural posture: how the case got to where it is. I usually put the procedure at the end of the facts.

Examples.
1. The lower court granted summary judgment for the defendant because . .
.

2. The lower court dismissed the case because of lack of personal jurisdiction over the defendant.

Reasoning: The reasoning is how the court answered the issue by applying the law to the facts. This is the most important part of your brief because finding the court's reasoning helps you improve your legal reasoning abilities. The more specific you are in establishing the court's reasoning, the more you will polish your legal reasoning skills. The most important thing is not what the law is, but why the law is the way it is. (The most important question in law school is "why?".)

Start your reasoning with the rule the court used. (Make sure you have found the correct rule, and write it clearly.) Then, explain how the court interpreted the rule. Finally, show how the court applied the law to the facts. (I have more on reasoning in the next section of this chapter.)

Holding: The holding answers the issue. It is the court's legal decision. It is a precedent (a rule) that you can apply to later cases. Make sure the rule is specific, but also easy to understand.

Examples.
1. The fact that a person was secretly drunk when entering into a contract does not negate that person's acceptance if a reasonable person would have thought that he had accepted the contract.
2. No, the evidence established that Jones's failure to stop at the traffic light was not the cause-in-fact of the accident as a matter of law. (Not all holdings will make good rules for future use.)
3. A landlord did not breach the lease with the tenant when he failed to provide electricity and heat to tenant's apartment for 24 hours during a cold streak because the failure was due to bad weather that prevented him from getting necessary parts.

Don't forget about the post-reading stage when briefing cases. (See above)

A few other bits of advice:

1. Skim the case, then read it in depth multiple times.
2. When reading cases be detail-oriented. For example, determine which facts are material and which ones aren't. (A key part of being a successful law student is being able to separate what is important from what is not.) Does the outcome of the case hinge on a a specific detail? Read word-by-word; every word might be material. Watch for grammar; a comma in a particular place can completely change the meaning.
3. Ask how the court has interpreted the law. Broadly or narrowly? Did the court follow a pre-existing rule or did it overrule or distinguish a previous case? Has the court synthesized a rule or part of a rule from previous cases?
4. As I said in the section on reading texts, engage with the text. Connect the case with prior cases. Question the court's reasoning. Develop questions about the text. (Why did the court read the precedent in the way that it did? Why did the court interpret this fact the way it did? Why did the court distinguish this prior case?) How would this case apply if this fact were changed (hypotheticals)?
5. Make sure you understand all terms the court uses? (Use a general dictionary and a legal dictionary.)
6. When possible, picture the case's facts in your head.

Exercise

Analyze (brief) the following case, using the format set forth above. (This case has been edited to focus on the main issue. Most case books edit the cases.)

796 S.W.2d 1 (1990)
HUMANA OF KENTUCKY, INC., d/b/a Humana Hospital Audubon, Movant,
v.
PAMELA V. SEITZ, Respondent.

Supreme Court of Kentucky.
September 27, 1990.

STEPHENS, Chief Justice.

The issue we decide on this appeal is whether the evidence presented by the respondent-plaintiff in this case satisfied the threshold requirements of the tort of outrageous conduct, so as to justify submitting the case to a jury. The Court of Appeals answered the question in the affirmative. We disagree with the Court of Appeals and reverse its decision.

On March 11, 1985, respondent, while a patient at movant's hospital, gave birth to a stillborn fetus. On August 8, 1985, respondent filed a suit in the Jefferson Circuit Court, claiming negligence, breach of contract, and intentional infliction of emotional distress. Following pretrial discovery, the trial judge granted a summary judgment to Humana [the hospital], declaring that the acts of the hospital staff were not "so extreme in degree as to go beyond all possible bounds of decency, [as] to be regarded as atrocious, and utterly intolerable in a civilized community." The trial court also found that the acts of the Humana staff did not take place over an extended period of time. The trial court relied primarily on Craft v. Rice, Ky., 671 S.W.2d 247 (1984).

The Court of Appeals reversed the summary judgment and remanded the case with directions that the trial court should go forward with discovery and trial. The appellate court believed Craft does not require that the alleged outrageous conduct extend over a long period of time. It relied on two cases, Rockhill v. Pollard, 259 Or. 54, 485 P.2d 28 (1971), and Hall v. May Department Stores Co., 292 Or. 131, 637 P.2d 126 (1981), for the proposition that the relationship between the parties must be examined as an element of the tort. The court in Rockhill made a determination of the special duties owed by a physician to a patient. Similarly, the Court of Appeals in this case stated that the "special duties owed by a nurse to a patient are important" in deciding what behavior may be found to be extreme or outrageous.

Respondent was admitted to Humana Hospital on February 28, 1985, as a result of pregnancy complications involving a ruptured membrane. On March 10, 1985, she began experiencing pain, which she believed to be the beginning of labor. A nurse examined Ms. Seitz and informed her that she was not in labor. The pains, however, continued through the night until the early morning of March 11, 1985. Respondent contacted nurses through the bed communicator unit in her room. She was sedated and was given pain relief medicine. At about 6 a.m., she attempted to contact the nurses, but the light on her bed unit failed to come on. She "believed" the unit had been disconnected by the nursing staff. She was served breakfast and had her vital signs checked shortly after 7 a.m. After the nurse left, she felt a sharp abdominal pain. She thought she had to "go to the bathroom." Her roommate advised her not to get out of bed, but rather to use a bedpan. The roommate shut the door to the room, and at the same time, respondent began delivering the baby into the bedpan. The roommate attempted to notify the nurses on respondent's intercom, and when it did not work, she used her bedside unit. Receiving no answer, the roommate then went to the hall and yelled for help. In several minutes a cleaning woman responded.

Several minutes after that, nurses arrived and rendered assistance. During this time, one of the nurses shouted to respondent, ordering her to "shut up" because she was disturbing other patients. A few minutes later, the respondent's obstetrician came into the room, on a regular visit, and examined the fetus and respondent. He pronounced the baby dead.

A nurse wrapped the deceased baby in a sheet, and the respondent inquired where the nurse was going to take the baby. According to the respondent, the nurse said, "Honey, we dispose of them right here at the hospital."

Respondent's physician testified that, based on the history of the incident and his personal observation, the nurse "failed to demonstrate the amount of compassion that a nurse should demonstrate toward a patient. I think that it was mishandled, and that amount of trauma, emotional trauma, could have been avoided."

Based on this evidence, respondent claims that the hospital, through the conduct of its nursing staff, is liable for outrageous conduct in the handling of the above-described episode.

This Court adopted the tort of outrageous conduct in . . . Craft v. Rice, supra. In that case, Albert and Irene Craft, husband and wife, lived in the weighmaster's house of Ashland Coal Company, where Albert worked weighing coal and coal trucks. He was indicted for second-degree forgery for allegedly falsifying weigh tickets, but was acquitted. For nearly three months, presumably prior to trial, Rice, a former sheriff, kept Irene Craft under surveillance at work and at home, telling her on the "CB" radio that he was going to put Albert in jail. He allegedly drove close to her, forcing her to change traffic lanes. He allegedly talked on the CB radio to Albert Craft. This alleged harassment led to mental anguish on the part of Albert, and chronic diarrhea, colitis and nervousness on the part of Irene. No physical touching occurred. The gravamen of the Crafts' complaint against Rice was interference with their rights, causing emotional distress.

In adopting this new tort, we recognized the elements of proof necessary to sustain the cause of action:

1) the wrongdoer's conduct must be intentional or reckless;

2) the conduct must be outrageous and intolerable in that it offends against the generally accepted standards of decency and morality;

3) there must be a causal connection between the wrongdoer's conduct and the emotional distress; and

4) the emotional distress must be severe.

Craft, 671 S.W.2d at 249.

Based on the facts as stated, we declared as a matter of law that the conduct of Rice "is a deviation from all reasonable bounds of decency and is utterly intolerable in a civilized community. It qualifies as harassment intended to cause extreme emotional distress." Craft, 671 S.W.2d at 250.

In Craft we adopted Restatement (Second) of Torts, § 46 (1965), as part of the common law of this Commonwealth. That section provides:

"§ 46. Outrageous Conduct Causing Severe Emotional Distress

(1) One who by extreme and outrageous conduct intentionally or recklessly causes severe emotional distress to another is subject to liability for such emotional distress, and if bodily harm to the other results from it, for such bodily harm."

The question we must decide, therefore, is whether, as a matter of law, taking the evidence of the respondent-plaintiff as being true, that evidence falls within the purview of § 46 and the four criteria we set out in Craft. Is it sufficient to satisfy the threshold requirements for the tort of outrageous conduct? We believe the answer is "no."

55

The salient "facts" relied on by respondent are as follows:

1) her belief that her intercom was disconnected;

2) the lapse of 12-15 minutes between the beginning of delivery and when nurses actually arrived in respondent's room;

3) a nurse telling respondent to "shut up"; and

4) a nurse telling respondent that the baby would be disposed of in the hospital.

In Comment d of § 46 of the Restatement, supra, it is stated:

"d. Extreme and outrageous conduct. It has not been enough that the defendant has acted with an intent which is tortious ..., or that he has intended to inflict emotional distress, or even that his conduct has been characterized by `malice,'.... Liability has been found only where the conduct has been so outrageous in character, and so extreme in degree, as to go beyond all possible bounds of decency, and to be regarded as atrocious, and utterly intolerable in a civilized community."

Restatement (Second) of Torts, § 46 Comment d (emphasis added).

Certainly, as respondent's physician testified, the nurse's conduct showed a lack of compassion. We agree that a little more patience and TLC would have been desirable. However, after examining the facts as alleged by the respondent, we believe they describe conduct that falls short of the standards set out above.

First, there is no proof that the intercom by respondent's bed was turned off. Admittedly, it was only her "belief" that such occurred. "Belief" is not evidence and does not create an issue of material fact. A plaintiff must present affirmative evidence in order to defeat a properly supported motion for summary judgment. Anderson v. Liberty Lobby, Inc., 477 U.S. 242, 106 S.Ct. 2505, 91 L.Ed.2d 202 (1986).

The delay in time before a nurse arrived may well be negligence, but it is hardly intentional, outrageous, or reckless conduct. All other evidence indicated that the nursing staff carefully and regularly cared for respondent from the time she began suffering pain. The time lapse, per se, would only tend to show negligence, not the tortious conduct alleged here.

The evidence of the nurse telling respondent to "shut up" likewise is not of such a nature to show that the offending nurse intentionally or recklessly caused emotional distress. Respondent was obviously distressed at giving premature birth, and the curt admonition, under the circumstances, was necessary to calm respondent, and to limit noise to prevent disturbance and discomfort to other patients in the hospital. Finally, telling respondent that the baby would be disposed of in the hospital is cold, callous, and lacking sensitivity, but it certainly is not part of a pattern of conduct that "is beyond all decency."

The evidence relied on shows, at worst, a lack of compassion and lack of taste, but certainly does not comport with the criteria in Craft and in the Restatement § 46.

In conclusion, although we hold that the trial court properly granted the motion for summary judgment, we do not understand Craft to hold that outrageous conduct must extend over a long period of time in order to constitute the tort. In this case, we find that the conduct in question was not intentional, outrageous, or reckless under the standards set out in Craft and the Restatement, supra.

The decision of the Court of Appeals is reversed, and the case is remanded to the trial court for entry of a judgment consistent with this opinion.

LEIBSON, Justice, dissenting.

Respectfully, I dissent.

The trial court erred in granting summary judgment under the facts of this case. In Craft v. Rice, Ky., 671 S.W.2d 247 (1984), we adopted Section 46 of the Restatement (Second) of Torts. Comment h to that section provides:

"It is for the court to determine, in the first instance, whether the defendant's conduct may reasonably be regarded as so extreme and outrageous as to permit recovery, or whether it is necessarily so. Where reasonable men may differ, it is for the jury, subject to the control of the court, to determine whether, in the particular case, the conduct has been sufficiently extreme and outrageous to result in liability." [Emphasis added]

In Craft the harassment of Mr. and Mrs. Craft continued over a period of three months. Craft does not, however, require the acts to take place over an extended period of time in order to make a case for intentional infliction of emotional distress. The acts of harassment must be intentional and substantial, but there is no time frame-work necessarily controlling. The state of the law in this area is still developing, and we must look to the facts in each case. Harassment cannot be proved by a single spontaneous act but here there was evidence from which a jury might infer multiple acts constituting a continuous, intentional course of action.

Ms. Seitz had been in the hospital for ten days with complications with her "high risk" pregnancy. There was evidence the staff had come to view her as a problem patient. The Majority states that there was no proof that her intercom had been turned off and the delay of the nursing staff for 12-15 minutes may have been negligent "but it is hardly intentional, outrageous or reckless conduct." Eleven nurses testified in pre-trial depositions that the call light was in fact working. If that was the case, then the failure of any of the nurses to respond to her call for help for 12-15 minutes may well suggest intentional harassment of the patient. Ms. Seitz had already given birth to a stillborn child in a bedpan. A 12-15 minute wait for nursing assistance may well be a veritable "life-time" under these circumstances.

An Arizona case, Lucchesi v. Frederic N. Stimmell, M.D., Ltd., 149 Ariz. 76, 716 P.2d 1013 (1986), is analogous. A patient with a "high risk" pregnancy was transported to a specific facility to be assisted by a doctor with special medical skills. There was a dispute as to whether the doctor had assured the patient's private physician that he would be waiting for her when she was transported. The doctor failed to come to the hospital despite the fact that he had been advised of the patient's complications after she arrived. Since the doctor was not present, a first-year intern and a third-year resident without experience with this type of complication had to deliver the baby. Not only was the child stillborn but was decapitated during the birth process as a result of the resident's procedure. Later, when Dr. Stimmell arrived at the hospital he failed to reveal to the patient what had happened during the delivery. She found out later from her own doctor. The Arizona Supreme Court, sitting en banc, reversed the grant of summary judgment on the plaintiff's claim for intentional infliction of emotional distress and held:

"[T]he evidence concerning Dr. Stimmell's conduct before, during and after the birth of the Lucchesis' child created a factual issue so that a jury should have had an opportunity to decide whether defendant's conduct was outrageous ... the existence of several factual inconsistencies in the record was sufficient to have precluded the entry of summary judgment [citation omitted]." Id. 149 Ariz. at 80, 716 P.2d at 1017.

Here, a jury should have been given the opportunity to decide whether the conduct of the nursing staff before, during and after the birth of Ms. Seitz' child was outrageous. A jury should also have been allowed to consider the special relationship of patient-nurse and whether the nursing staff had knowledge of the patient's susceptibility to emotional distress per comment e and comment f of the Restatement.

I would affirm the decision of the Court of Appeals.

Sample Brief

HUMANA OF KENTUCKY, INC. v. PAMELA V. SEITZ
Supreme Court of Kentucky. September 27, 1990. 796 S.W.2d 1 (1990).

[Do you know what 796 S.2d 1 means?]

Issues:

1. Whether the evidence presented by the respondent-plaintiff in this case satisfied the threshold requirements of the tort of outrageous conduct, so as to justify submitting the case to a jury.
2. Whether outrageous conduct must extend over a long period of time in order to constitute intentional infliction of emotional harm.

[1. Don't be concerned if you worded the issues differently than I did. The important thing is to get the substance of the issue correctly. 2. You can use the language of the court for the issue in your brief. However, don't use the court's language if you think the court stated it incorrectly (this does happen) or if you can write it better. 3. I gave two issues in this case to demonstrate that cases often had multiple issues. The second issue was not important for the outcome of this case before the Kentucky Supreme Court. (Can you see why?) However, the case in the Court of Appeals hinged on this issue. The second issue might be relevant for a later case that involves the length of the outrageous conduct.]

Facts:

This case involves the alleged tort of outrageous conduct. Pamela Seitz was admitted to a hospital as a result of pregnancy complications involving a ruptured membrane. Her pain continued throughout the night, and she delivered a still born baby. She alleged the following as outrageous conduct by the hospital staff:

1) her belief that her intercom was disconnected;
2) the lapse of 12-15 minutes between the beginning of delivery and when nurses actually arrived in respondent's room;
3) a nurse telling respondent to "shut up"; and
4) a nurse telling respondent that the baby would be disposed of in the hospital.

The trial judge granted a summary judgment to the hospital, declaring that the acts of its staff were not "so extreme in degree as to go beyond all possible bounds of decency, [as] to be regarded as atrocious, and utterly intolerable in a civilized community." The trial court also found that the acts of the Humana staff did not take place over an extended period of time. The Court of Appeals reversed the summary judgment and remanded the case with directions that the trial court should go forward with discovery and trial. The appellate court believed that outrageous conduct does not have to extend over a long period of time.

[1. It is often difficult to decide what facts you should include in your brief, especially when the case is factually complicated like this one. You don't want to make the facts too long, but you also don't want to leave out any material facts. Remember that material facts are the facts that determine the outcome. 2. Notice how the procedural posture helps you better understand what the court is doing.]

Holdings:

1. The evidence presented by the respondent-plaintiff in this case did not satisfy the requirements of the tort of outrageous conduct, so as to justify submitting the case to a jury.

2. Outrageous conduct need not extend over a long period of time in order to constitute intentional infliction of emotional harm.

[Remember the holding answers the issue.]

Reasoning:

The court applies the following test to determine intentional infliction of emotional harm:

1) the wrongdoer's conduct must be intentional or reckless;

2) the conduct must be outrageous and intolerable in that it offends against the generally accepted standards of decency and morality;

3) there must be a causal connection between the wrongdoer's conduct and the emotional distress; and

4) the emotional distress must be severe.

Only the outrageous conduct prong was relevant in this case. The court defined outrageous conduct as "One who by extreme and outrageous conduct intentionally or recklessly causes severe emotional distress to another is subject to liability for such emotional distress, and if bodily harm to the other results from it, for such bodily harm." The court added, "d. Extreme and outrageous conduct. It has not been enough that the defendant has acted with an intent which is tortious ..., or that he has intended to inflict emotional distress, or even that his conduct has been characterized by `malice,'.... Liability has been found only where the conduct has been so outrageous in character, and so extreme in degree, as to go beyond all possible bounds of decency, and to be regarded as atrocious, and utterly intolerable in a civilized community."

Based on these criteria, the court held that the hospital's conduct was not outrageous. The court stated that 1) a plaintiff must present affirmative evidence in order to defeat a properly supported motion for summary judgment; 2) the delay in time before a nurse arrived may well be negligence, but it is hardly intentional, outrageous, or reckless conduct; 3) the evidence of the nurse telling respondent to "shut up" likewise is not of such a nature to show that the offending nurse intentionally or recklessly caused emotional distress., 4) telling respondent that the baby would be disposed of in the hos-pital is cold, callous, and lacking sensitivity, but it certainly is not part of a pattern of conduct that "is beyond all decency."

[1. My reasoning is longer than most reasoning sections in case briefs. However, I wanted to give you a full picture of the court's reasoning. Even if your reasoning section is more concise, you should have fully understood the court's reasoning when you read the case. If you didn't, you are not developing your legal reasoning properly. 2. Notice how I organized the reasoning. I started by giving the general law, then I gave the more specific law. Finally, I showed how the court applied the law to the facts. This is the basis of legal reasoning: present the law, explain the law, apply the law to the facts in detail.]

Dissent: The dissent felt that the issue of outrageous conduct was for the jury to decide. (Can you say why?)

[Comparing the reasoning of the majority opinion with the dissenting opinion will help you hone your reasoning skills.]

Exercises

1. What are the main parts of a case analysis (brief)? Why is each part important? Which part helps you refine your legal reasoning skills the most?
2. Why is reading concurrences and dissents important?

III. Identifying the Type of Reasoning the Court is Using.

The above presents a typical example of a law school brief. However, I have added an additional step to the analysis, which will help you further develop your reasoning skills. You can improve your legal reasoning by identifying the type of reasoning the court is using.

There are five types of reasoning that judges employ to adjudicate cases: 1) rule-based reasoning (deductive reasoning), 2) synthesis (inductive reasoning), 3) analogical reasoning, 4) distinguishing cases, and 5) policy-based reasoning. Judges generally use these in combination. (see exercise below.)

1. Rule-Based Reasoning.

In rule-based reasoning, you take a rule (a statute, a case holding, or an administrative regulation) and apply it to the facts. (This is deductive reasoning–reasoning from the general to the specific.) Then, you come to a conclusion.

Example.

Facts: A department store security guard told Max, a suspected shoplifter, to stay in his office while he got his manager. The guard locked Max in, and Max heard the lock turn. Max got up, and he tried to turn the door knob, but he found that the door was locked. When the manager and guard came back, they discovered that Max had a receipt in his shirt pocket. They told him he could go. Max sues for false imprisonment.

Rule: A false imprisonment occurs when 1) the defendant kept plaintiff within boundaries set up by the defendant; 2) the defendant intended to imprison the plaintiff by keeping the plaintiff within those boundaries; 3) the boundaries actually kept the plaintiff from leaving; and 3) the plaintiff knew he was being imprisoned.

Application: 1) the guard satisfied part 1 by locking Max in his office. 2) Locking the door demonstrated that the guard intended to imprison Max within the room. 3) Locking the door prevented Max from leaving. 4) Max was aware of the imprisonment because he heard the door lock, and he tried the door knob.

Conclusion: Since all four conjunctive elements are satisfied, a false imprisonment occurred.

2. Reasoning by Analogy.

Reasoning by analogy involves finding similarities. Reasoning by analogy in the law occurs when one argues that the facts of the precedent case are like the facts of the present case so that the rule of the precedent case should apply to the present case. (The facts of case A are like the facts of case B, so the rule from case A should apply to case B.) The two cases are rarely exactly the same; reasoning by analogy is a question of degree. The writer must convince the reader that the facts of the two cases are similar enough that the rule from the precedent case should apply to the present case.

Example.

Precedent case: A court held that knocking a hat off of someone's head was a battery because the hat was connected to the person.

New case: The defendant knocked a food tray out of plaintiff's hands. Was this a battery?

Analysis: Knocking a food tray out of someone's hands is like knocking a hat off of someone's head because both involve an item connected to the plaintiff. Therefore, there was a battery in the new case.

3. Distinguishing Cases.

Distinguishing cases is the opposite of reasoning by analogy. In distinguishing cases, one argues that the facts of the precedent case are not like the facts of the present case so that the rule from the precedent case does not apply to the present case. (The facts of case A are not like the facts of case B, so the rule from case A should not apply to case B.)

Example.

Precedent case: A court held that knocking a hat off of someone's head was a battery because the hat was connected to the person.

New case: The defendant knocked plaintiff's hat off a table. Is this a battery?

Analysis: Knocking a hat off a table is not like knocking a hat off a person's head because the hat in the second case is not connected with the plaintiff.

4. Reasoning by Policy.

With policy based-reasoning, the writer argues that applying a particular rule to a case would create a precedent that is good for society. Policy-based reasoning can also be combined with reasoning by analogy. For instance, one can argue that the policy behind the rule in the precedent case also applies to the present case so the rule from the precedent case should also apply to the present case.

Example.

Facts: A person owed a tiger, and he kept it in a secure cage. The tiger escaped and badly injured the plaintiff. The plaintiff cannot prove the owner was negligent. Should the plaintiff be able to recover from the tiger owner?

Policy: An earlier case had held that a land owner who kept explosives on his property was strictly liable to his neighbor when the explosives exploded injuring him. The court reasoned that one who keeps dangerous items on his property should be strictly liable if those dangerous items cause harm.

Application: The policy behind the tiger case should be the same as the policy behind the explosives case. Both cases involved something that was very dangerous, and the defendants should be liable when the danger occurs. Therefore, the plaintiff in the new case should be able to recover based on strict liability.

5. Inductive Reasoning.

Inductive reasoning is reasoning from the specific to the general. Lawyers use inductive reasoning to synthesize rules. In synthesizing rules, lawyers take holdings from several cases and by synthesizing those specific cases, they come up with a general rule. To synthesize a rule, look at the similarities among the facts of the precedent cases and the differences among the facts of those cases. Then, evaluate how those similarities and differences affected the holdings. Also, look at the reasoning behind the holdings. One can also synthesize other texts. For example, a writer can synthesize arguments from three law review article to create a new argument.

Example.

Synthesize a rule from the following cases. Put the elements in a logical order.

Case 1. The court refused to find for the plaintiff under a theory of intentional infliction of emotional harm because the plaintiff had not proven that the defendant's conduct caused the plaintiff's emotional distress.

Case 2. The court refused to rule for the plaintiff under a theory of intentional infliction of emotional distress because the plaintiff had not suffered emotional distress.

Case 3. The court refused to give the plaintiff recovery under intentional infliction of emotional distress because the plaintiff had not proven that the plaintiff's conduct was intentional.

Case 4. The court did not allow recovery for the plaintiff for intentional infliction of emotional distress because the defendant's conduct was not extreme and outrageous.

Answer

This is a simple exercise. You should synthesis a rule for intentional infliction of emotional distress based on the four cases. Each case gives you one of the elements. First, you must determine whether the test is conjunctive (all factors required for recovery), disjunctive (only one factor required for recovery), or a weighing test (weigh the factors). Next, you must put the factors in a logical order. Usually, this will be the order that the factors generally occur.

First, each case denied recovery because one factor was not satisfied. Since all the elements are required, this makes the test conjunctive. Since outrageous conduct precedes the other factors this should go first. The damages or harm generally goes last. Causation generally goes right before the damages or harm. Synthesized rule: To establish intentional infliction of emotional distress, a plaintiff must prove that 1) the defendant's conduct was extreme and outrageous, 2) the defendant's conduct was intentional, 3) it caused 4) the plaintiff emotional distress. (Don't be concerned if your wording is not the same as mine. The important thing is that you found the four elements.)

When reading cases, you should always determine the type of legal reasoning the judge is using. This is one way for you to attain deep reading and deep learning.

Exercise

1. What are the five types of legal reasoning? Define each one in detail. Try to give new examples of each one.

Exercise

Identify the type of legal reasoning at each bolded letter.

In case I, an exotic animal lover kept a tiger on his property, being very careful to make sure it did not escape. The tiger escaped and bite a neighbor causing him to incur $500 in medical costs. The court held that the tiger owner was liable for the damages under strict liability on the ground that one who owns a wild animal that escapes and causes personal injury should be liable regardless of fault because the owner brought the wild animal into the neighborhood knowing it was dangerous. (←A) In case II, a person owned a pit bull. The pit bull escaped despite the fact that the owner was very careful to keep it caged up, and it bite a neighbor causing her to incur $500 in hospital bills. The court held that the pit bull owner was strictly liable for the personal injuries because a pit bull is like a tiger. (←**B**) In case III, grandma owned a sweet french poodle named Fluffy, which had never even growled at another person before the incident. When a loud helicopter flew overhead, Fluffy became frightened, causing him to bite a neighbor who incurred $500 in medical bills. The court held that Grandma was not liable for the neighbor's medical expenses on the grounds that an owner of a poodle, unlike the owner of a tiger or a pit bull, had no reason to know that Fluffy might bite someone and that someone who has no reason to know of a danger should not be held strictly liable and a french poodle is not like a pit bull or a tiger. (←**C**) Based on cases I, II, and III: An owner of an animal that has reason to know that animal might be dangerous can be held strictly liable for personal injury caused by that animal. (←**D**)

Answers. A. Reasoning by policy (the court didn't have a precedent on this issue so it was forced to make its decision based on policy), B. Reasoning by analogy (a pit bull is like a tiger because it is a dangerous animal so the rule from case I applies to case II), C. Reasoning by policy and distinguishing cases (a poodle is not like a tiger or a pit bull so the rule from cases I and II should not apply to case III), D. Inductive reasoning (rule synthesis; you are taking the holdings from the three cases and coming up with a broad rule that is consistent with all three cases).

I deal with legal reasoning in detail in my book, Think Like a Lawyer: Legal Reasoning for Law Students and Business Professionals (ABA Pub. 2013). The book also contains many exercises to help you understand the five types of legal reasoning in depth.

Notes

1. I have based these categories on Michael Hunter Schwartz's three phases of self-regulated learning. Michael Hunter Schwartz, *Teaching Law Students to Be Self-Regulated Learners*, 2003 MICH ST. DCL L. REV. 447, 454-55.

2. *Id.* at 456.

3. *Id.* at 457; Peter Dewitz, *Legal Education: A Problem of Learning from Text*, 23 N.Y.U. L. REV. L. & SOC. CHANGE 225, 228 (1997) (Strategic readers "set a purpose for reading, self-question, search for important information, make inferences, summarize, and monitor the

developing meaning."). Professor Christensen notes that low performing students employ default reading strategies (basic reading strategies: moving through the text in a linear manner, para-phrasing, rereading, noting certain structural elements of the text, underlining text, making margin notes) much more than high performing students. Leah M Christensen, Legal Reading and Success in Law School: An Empirical Study, 30 Seattle University Law Review 603, 644 (2007).

4. Christensen, *supra* at 608 (2007).

5. Schwartz, *supra* at 458.

6. *Id.* at 458-59.

7. TERRY DOYLE & TODD D. ZAKRAJSEK, THE NEW SCIENCE OF LEARNING: HOW TO LEARN IN HARMONY WITH YOUR BRAIN 79 (2013).

8. Reza Zabihi & Mojtaba Pordel, *An Investigation of Critical Reading in Reading Textbooks: A Qualitative Analysis*, https://files.eric.ed.gov/fulltext/EJ1066522.pdf at 82; *see also* Diane F. Halpern, *Teaching Critical Thinking for Transfer across Domains: Dispositions, Skills, Structure Training, and Metacognitive Monitoring*, 53 AM. PSYCH. 449, 450-51 (1998) ("Critical thinking is purposeful, reasoned, and goal-directed. It is the kind of thinking involved in solving problems, formulating inferences, calculating likelihoods, and making decisions.").

9. Brian P. Coppola, *Progress in Practice: Using Concepts from Motivational and Self-Regulated Learning Research to Improve Chemistry Instruction*, 63 NEW DIRECTIONS FOR TEACHING AND LEARNING: UNDERSTANDING SELF-REGULATED LEARNING 87, 92 (1995).

10. Zabihi & Pordel, *supra* at 81.

11. Schwartz, *supra* at 460.

12. Coppola, supra at 92.

13. Professors Oatley and Djikic write, "Novice readers concentrate at the word and sentence level, as compared with experts who think about larger-scale structures and their possible meanings." Keith Oatley & Maja Djikic, *Writing as Thinking*," 12 REV. GEN. PSYCH. 9, 13-14 (2008). For expert readers, "Reading a paragraph involves finding the main idea of the paragraph and how it is related to other paragraphs. Structural reading can be used to locate the main paragraphs in a text. Having understood the main ideas in a paragraph, good readers are able to connect them meaningfully to their own situations and experiences." Zabihi & Pordel, *supra* at 82.

14. Christensen, *Legal Reading*, *supra* at 609.

15. Schwartz, *supra* at 460-61.

16. *Id.* at 462.

17. The emphasis here is on reasonable. Outlandish arguments don't win.

Chapter Four
How to Become A Metacognitive Learner

Chapter Goals.

1. To introduce metacognition, and show how it can make you a better learner.
2. To introduce the concepts of metacognition.
3. To introduce the three types of metacognitive knowledge: metacognitive declarative knowledge, metacognitive procedural knowledge, and metacognitive conditional knowledge.
4. To explain regulation of cognition.
5. To show you how to develop your metacognitive skills.

A recent study has shown that most law students lack metacognitive skills (defined below).[1] These authors assert, "The data demonstrates that top law students—hardworking, overachieving college graduates with high IQs—do not have well-developed metacognitive skills."[2] Similarly, the Carnegie Report (an important study of law school education) proclaimed: "the essential goal of professional schools must be to form practitioners who are aware of what it takes to be competent in their chosen domain and equips them with the reflective capacity and motivation to pursue genuine expertise. They must become 'metacognitive' about their learning . . ."[3]

I want you to become a metacognitive learner so that you can reach the fourth stage of learning (self-authoring) that I mentioned in the preface. (Your response: A what? I never heard of that before. I'm not sure I want to be a meta anything.) Learning metacognition is not hard; you just have to change how you view learning and start to take control of your learning.

I. Introduction to Metacognition.

Metacognition involves assessing and controlling your thinking. The actual learning stage is cognitive thinking, while the level above that one is the metacognitive level, which controls the cognitive level. Think about your mind as a supercomputer that controls several subsidiary computers, which do the actual work. The supercomputer is metacognition, while the subsidiary computers are cognition. (Got it? Now let me confuse you with some further

71

explanation of metacognition.)

Metacognition is thinking about thinking.[4] It includes "both knowledge of one's knowledge, processes, cognitive and affective states, and the ability to consciously and deliberately monitor and regulate one's knowledge, process, cognitive and affective states."[5] (Got it. Two parts. Knowledge of thinking, etc. and ability to control and monitor one's thinking, etc.) "Metacognition involves the understanding of how a task is performed."[6] It also allows "learners to understand and monitor their cognitive processes."[7] (There's the two parts again.) In sum, "Metacognition refers to awareness of one's own knowledge— what one does and doesn't know—and one's ability to understand, control, and manipulate one's cognitive processes. It includes knowing when and where to use particular strategies for learning and problem-solving as well as how and why to use specific strategies. Metacognition is the ability to use prior knowledge to plan a strategy for approaching a learning task, take necessary steps to problem solve, reflect on and evaluate results, and modify one's approach as needed."[8]

I have already taught you some metacognition without you knowing it. In Chapter Two, I taught you how to develop effective study habits. Knowledge of effective study habits is metacognition. Using those habits to study is cognition. Monitoring to determine whether you have used the study habits properly is metacognition. Similarly, in Chapter Three, I taught you how to be an effective reader. Knowledge of the effective reading process is metacognition. Using that process to read a text is cognition. Monitoring to determine whether you are reading effectively is metacognition. Knowing you should reflect on what you have learned is metacognition. Now is metacognition clearer?

Let's go into a little more detail. Metacognition regulates learning through a cognitive regulatory loop.[9] First, metacognition monitors the learning process. Then, based on that monitoring, metacognition controls the learning process.[10] Thus, metacognition, as I mentioned above, consists of two main subdivisions: knowledge of cognition and regulation of cognition (control).[11]

Knowledge of cognition consists of three parts: "[D]eclarative knowledge (knowledge about oneself as a learner—the factors that influence performance), procedural knowledge (knowledge about strategies and other procedures), and conditional knowledge (knowledge of why and when to use a particular strategy)."[12]

Metacognitive declarative knowledge "is information that one consults when thinking about a particular cognition."[13] It is a database, which contains "how we or other persons process various tasks, how well we performed on them, what we felt during the task processing, when, why, and what kind of strategies were used . . ., and what kind of goals people have when dealing with a task or a situation."[14] Some illustrations include how one should best manage tasks and how the availability of information affects the handling of a task.[15] For example, a problem solver needs to know when she lacks sufficient information to accomplish a task.[16] Likewise, knowledge of cognitive tasks also consists of how tasks, such as recall tasks and recognition tasks, differ.[17]

Self-knowledge, including one's strengths and weaknesses (what works best for you), is an important type of metacognitive declarative knowledge.[18] For example, it includes the self-knowledge that one is better at listening than reading.[19] Self-knowledge also encompasses knowledge of one's motivation, one's evaluation of one's ability to perform a task (self-efficacy), one's goals for the task (learning, attaining a good grade), and one's interest in and value for the task.[20] (There is motivation, self-efficacy, goals, values, and interests again. Can you see how everything I am talking about in this book fits together?) Self-knowledge helps individuals "attend to those procedures with higher probabilities of success."[21] (Isn't this part of self-efficacy?) Such self-knowledge, however, must be accurate; otherwise, you will have an inaccurate picture of yourself. (You need to be able to discern false praise from your teachers, parents, and others.) Similarly, faulty metacognitive declarative knowledge is usually hard to unlearn.[22] (In other words, it is hard to unlearn a poor strategy.) You need to be aware of cognitive illusions, such as illusions of knowing or cognitive biases.[23]

Metacognitive procedural knowledge ("knowledge how") concerns how humans perform cognitive tasks.[24] In other words, it involves strategies on how to solve problems. "Strategic knowledge is knowledge of general strategies for learning, thinking, and problem solving."[25] Strategies are "set[s] of mental processes" thinkers use to achieve a particular purpose."[26] For example, a strategy might involve a reading strategy (like we talked about in Chapter Three), a comprehension strategy, or a memorization strategy. An illustration of a learning strategy is to focus on the main points and rephrase them.[27] One can use general strategies across subject-matter domains (domain transfer), such as applying a strategy for reading a textbook in a literature class to reading a textbook in a science class.[28] Similarly, monitoring cognition as one reads is a general strategy.[29]

There are three principal groups of learning strategies: 1) rehearsal—"the strategy of repeating words or terns to be remembered over and over to oneself," 2) elaboration–"mnemonics for memory tasks as well as strategies for summarizing, paraphrasing, and selecting main ideas from texts," and 3) organizational–"outlining, concept mapping, and note taking, where the student makes connections between and among content elements."[30] Elaboration also includes generating examples.[31] Other strategies include how to set goals and subgoals, how to monitor cognition, and how to regulate cognition.[32] There are also general thinking strategies, such as means-ends strategies, deductive and inductive reasoning, etc.[33]

Metacognitive conditional knowledge concerns the application of strategies at the proper time and place and for the proper reason (when and how),[34] and it also involves both effectiveness and efficiency.[35] In other words, a thinker uses different tools and different strategies for different cognitive tasks, just as a carpenter uses a hammer or a saw in different situations.[36] To illustrate, "hypothetical–deductive reasoning is an appropriate strategy for medical problem solving whereas analogical or case-based reasoning may be more appropriate in many design domains such as architecture."[37] (I hope you recognize the importance of conditional knowledge. If you don't use the right tool (strategy, procedure), you won't get the right answer. Imagine a carpenter trying to hammer with a screw driver.) You should also employ metacognitive flexibility–the willingness to try different strategies with different problems–in connection with conditional knowledge.[38]

Here is an example of using metacognitive conditional knowledge in law school. You will be taught IRAC (Issue-Rule-Application-Conclusion) early in the first year as a method of organizing legal arguments. Conditional metacognitive knowledge concerns when you use IRAC. Do you use it in the fact section of a objective memorandum? Do you use it as a format to draft contracts? Do you use it when you draft a will? (The answer to these three questions is No!)

Now let's turn to regulation of cognition. Regulatory metacognitive skills control cognition.[39] Regulatory metacognitive skills include planning, monitoring ("strategies for . . . checking the implementation of the planned action"), and evaluating ("strategies for evaluating the outcome of task processing").[40] In addition, regulatory metacognitive skills include strategies for recapitulation and self-regulation, which "involve strategies for the appraisal of the whole endeavor with a task, of what happened from the beginning to the end of processing, the strengths and weaknesses, the causes of the outcomes, and what should be attended to in the future."[41] (In other words, recapitulation and self-regulation help improve future learning and other task handling.)

Planning is "the selection of appropriate strategies and the allocation of resources that affect one's learning performance."[42] Planning skills include setting goals, creating strategies, making predictions, and time and practical management.[43]

Monitoring, which I have mentioned before, is "one's on-line awareness of comprehension and task performance."[44] In other words, did the thinker achieve an accurate and proper result (metacomprehension–"the accuracy of metacognitive monitoring"), and did she use the best process to reach that result (was it efficient)?[45] The most basic monitoring skill is realizing that one does not understand something.[46] A more complex example concerns studying:

> consider a student preparing for an exam. As the student studies, she monitors her progress toward the goal of mastering the material. If her monitoring indicates that she has not yet mastered the material, she will likely restudy the material. If her monitoring indicates mastery has been accomplished, then that material is not selected for restudy. Therefore, accurate metacognitive monitoring is critical to effective regulation of study. If a person is not able to accurately differentiate well-learned material from less-learned material, he or she could waste time studying material that is already well learned, or worse, fail to restudy material that has not yet been adequately learned.[47]

Evaluating (reflecting), which I have also mentioned before, is appraising the products and regulatory processes of one's learning.[48] "Evaluating requires that the students critically look at whether the steps they took resulted in successful learning, whether the goals were met, and whether the anticipated obstacles were avoided or managed."[49] Moreover, "it is backward-looking in the sense that the student reflects on what she just did and how effective it was, and it is forward-looking in the sense that the student considers the implications of her experience for future learning activities."[50] After evaluating the learning, you should identify why the learning was successful or unsuccessful and, if unsuccessful, modify his learning strategy.[51]

Let's add one more thing to the metacognitive process–emotions. It makes sense that emotions affect learning. So, in addition to the metacognitive regulatory cognitive loop, there is a metacognitive regulatory affective loop, involving emotion, feelings, attitudes, and motivation, which furnishes the drive for self-regulation.[52] The regulatory affective loop exists because "success or failure in [the learning task] has implications for one's self and self-perception of competence."[53] (Relate this to the earlier discussion on self-efficacy and motivation.) Metacognitive emotions for the learning task are activity-related emotions, such as interest, boredom, hope, fear, and anxiety, which lead directly to action, and they can have a positive or negative effect.[54] Metacognitive feelings associated with the learning situation, such as feelings of knowing, difficulty, familiarity, confidence, and satisfaction, are not as urgent as with emotions, and they notify the thinker of the need for control decisions.[55] Concerning motivation, "there can be motivation in the form of personality traits that operates before the person gets involved with a task, motivation due to the task and situational factors, and motivation during and after the person's involvement with the task."[56] Metacognitive experiences "contribute to the person's motivation through their effect on causal attributions, on self-concept, and possibly on achievement goal orientations."[57] In sum, "the monitoring of the developing cognitive processing is reflected in the person's ME [metacognitive experiences]; the person, by making use of his/her MK [metacognitive knowledge], decodes the meaning of his/her ME—particularly of the metacognitive feelings—in order to make control decisions. These decisions are then implemented through cognitive and metacognitive strategies (i.e., MS)."[58]

Because emotions are part of learning, you need to be aware of and be able to control your negative emotions.[59] Monitoring involves being aware of negative emotions and negative self-talk, so that you will not let these interfere with learning and reinforce negative self-identity.[60] In addition, negative self-talk is often negative messages from others that you have internalized without critical examination.[61]

Summary of Metacognition

I. Knowledge of Cognition
    A. Declarative knowledge
    B. Procedural knowledge
    C. Conditional knowledge

II. Regulation of Cognition
    A. Planning
    B. Monitoring
    C. Evaluating/reflection

III. Regulatory Affective Loop

Exercises

1. What is metacognition?
2. Why is it important for your learning?
3. What is the difference between metacognition and cognition?
4. What are the two main parts of metacognition?
5. Have you used metacognition in your learning in the past, even though you were unaware of doing so? Think of several instances of your use of meta-cognition.
6. What is metacognitive declarative knowledge?
7. What is metacognitive procedural knowledge?
8. What is metacognitive conditional knowledge?
9. How do the three types metacognitive knowledge differ?
10. Why is metacognitive conditional knowledge important?
11. What is regulation of cognition? Why is it important?
12. What are the three types of regulation of cognition? Explain each?
13. Are emotions important in the metacognitive process? How do they affect learning?

II. How to Develop Your Metacognitive Skills.

You will be happy to hear that this part of the chapter is much easier than the previous part. I am mainly going to be asking you questions that will help you develop your metacognitive skills.

Here are some questions that will help you develop your learning skills:

Declarative Knowledge

1. Why is understanding the learning process important for your learning?
2. What skills are most important for a law student?
3. What skills are most important for a lawyer?
4. Do you have control over your learning process?
5. Do you set learning goals? Overall? For the semester? For each class? For each study session?
6. Are you an engaged learner? Do you understand what being an engaged

learner requires? Are you an effortful or lazy learner? Which type of learner usually gets higher grades? Are you an active or passive learner? Do you participate frequently in class? Do you reflect on what you have learned?

7. What are the strengths and weaknesses of your study techniques? Do you use a variety of study techniques?

8. Do you rely on learning techniques from college that are not effective for law school? Is rote learning a good strategy for law school?

9. How do you motivate yourself to learn? Are there other ways of motivating yourself you haven't tried?

10. What are you expected to learn in this class? (In other words, what do you think the professor expects from you?) How does this class differ from your other classes this semester? Do you believe you can succeed in this class? (What is this called?) Can a study group help you in this class? What do you expect to get from your study group?

11. Do you understand the different types of legal reasoning–deductive rea soning, reasoning by analogy, distinguishing cases, reasoning based on policy, synthesis?

12. How do you think of yourself as a learner? Have you been a successful learner in the past? Do you lack the talent to be a good learner? Are these views correct, or has someone else given these views to you?

13. Why do you want to be a lawyer? What interests you about law school?

Procedural Knowledge

1. Do you use learning techniques that have worked successfully in the past?

2. Do you always have clear goals when you tackle a problem?

3. Are you aware of the learning techniques you use while studying?

4. Do you read your notes the evening after class, or do you wait for right before the exam? Which approach is best for long-term learning? Do you review material every week, or do you wait for right before the exam? Which approach is best for long-term learning? Do you write your outlines gradually over the semester, or do you do them right before the exam? Which approach is better for long-term learning? Do you use graphic organizers (visual aids, such as charts, learning trees, outlines) to organize the materials you have learned in class? Why is it important to use graphic organizers?

5. Do you have an effective reading strategy? Do you read with a purpose? Do you understand the context of the reading before reading? Do you look at how a reading is organized before you start reading? Do you skim before reading? Do you reread passages you don't completely understand? Do you

relate the reading to prior knowledge? Do you question the reading? Do you talk back to the text? Do you think of alternatives to solutions, conclusions, or reasoning suggested in the text? Do you try to think of examples for what you have learned? Do you try to think of applications for what you have learned? Do you draw inferences from the text?

6. Do you have an effective case analysis strategy? Do you have a purpose when you read cases? Do you look at the case's context before you start reading? Do you skim cases, then read them in depth? Do you look for the different types of legal reasoning the judge is using? Can you discern material facts in cases? Can you spot issues in the cases and write them accurately? Why is the procedure below important? Can you find the holding of cases? Do you understand the reasoning of the cases? Do you question the court's reasoning? Do you try to find alternative reasoning for the cases's outcome (concurrence)? Do you write dissents to cases? How would this help you develop your reasoning skills? Do you test hypotheticals against the case? Do you relate the cases to other cases you have read? Do you draw inferences from the cases?

7. Do you test yourself (retrieval of knowledge) when you study?

8. How do you identify critical information? Is your method the most effective one?

9. Do you make connections between concepts? Are your methods the most effective ones?

10. How do you synthesize the cases you have read? Are you using the most effective method?

11. Do you use a journal for each class? What are the advantages of using a journal? What belongs in a journal?

12. Do you use knowledge or procedures from an area of knowledge in another area? What is this called?

13. How do you get rid of distractions when you study? Do you listen to music or watch television while studying? If yes, does this hurt your studying? Do you "surf" in class? If yes, does this hurt the attention you are able to give to the class?

14. Do you talk to the professor when you don't understand something? Why do some students talk to the professor a lot and some rarely? If you don't talk to the professor frequently, do you understand why you don't?

15. How would you teach another student to solve this problem (e.g., a contracts problem)?

Conditional Knowledge

1. Do you have a specific reason for using the note-taking techniques you use in class?
2. Do you have a specific reason for using the listening techniques you use in class?
3. Do you have a specific reason for using the learning techniques you use while studying?
4. Do you use your strengths to compensate for your weaknesses?
5. Can you motivate yourself to learn when you need to learn?
6. Do you use different learning techniques depending on the situation?
7. Do you know what learning techniques are most effective for a particular task?
8. Do you know when you should use different approaches to problem-solving?

Planning

1. Do you set learning goals for tasks?
2. Do you divide your studying into small units for a task so that it is most effective?
3. Do you pace yourself (spaced study) on a task so that you have enough time to study and so that you can keep up your attention?
4. Do you ask yourself questions about the material to be learned in a task?
5. Do you ask yourself questions about how much you already know about the subject matter to be learned?
6. How will you organize this task? Are there better methods to organize this task?
7. How did you handle self-efficacy for this task? Did you believe you could do the task?
8. How did you motivate yourself to do this task? Are these methods effective, or do you have to develop better ways to motivate yourself?
9. Did you set growth goals for this task?

Monitoring

1. How do you track the progress of your learning?
2. Do you make sure you are learning when you are in class? Are you giving the professor your full attention? Can you learn everything without giving the teacher your full attention? Do you ask questions when you don't understand something? If not, why are you not asking questions?

3. While studying, do you ask yourself periodically whether you are meeting your learning goals?

4. Once a week, do you ask yourself how well you are doing in your classes?

5. While studying, are you aware whether you are learning the material?

6. When you are reading, are you skimming or are you truly understanding the material?

7. How do you determine errors in your reasoning? Are your methods effective?

Evaluating

1. Do you ask yourself whether you are getting everything you can out of law school?

2. Do you ask yourself whether you have accomplished your goals when you finish studying or finish a task?

3. Do you ask yourself whether you have used the best techniques to study the material or solve the problem (including efficiency)?

4. Do you ask yourself whether you have considered all learning techniques?

5. Do you ask yourself whether you have attained the proper or best result? After you get back a test, do you think how you might have done better? After you get back a paper, do you think about how you might have written the paper better?

6. Have you asked yourself whether your evaluation of your work coincides with your professor's? If your evaluation of your work doesn't coincide with your professor's, why doesn't it?

7. Do you evaluate whether you've added to your growth goals?

8. Is it good or bad to make errors in law school? Can you learn from your errors?

9. How do you deal with failure?

10. What can you learn from failure?

11. Are you good at setting goals?

12. Do you jump to preliminary conclusions that are different from the correct answer? Does this cause you to come up with the wrong answer? Does this make you less efficient?

You probably said that you do not do many of things I asked you about in the above questions, especially if you are just starting law school. If you don't do these things, start doing them now. Develop learning habits. It takes time to become a better learner, but it is worthwhile. Then, answer these questions again at the middle of your first semester and at the end. This is a method of evaluating your learning skills.

Keeping a learning journal, as I recommended in Chapter Two, is also a great way to learn metacognition. Use the questions I just gave you. In particular, reflect on how your learning has improved as you've practiced the skills in this book and what you still need to improve.

In addition, you can also develop your metacognitive skills by putting yourself in the shoes of others. For example, assume you are writing an open objective memorandum for your legal writing class. Ask yourself: how would my legal writing professor critique my research strategy? How would my legal writing professor critique my analysis? What will my legal writing professor think about how I organized my memo?

Or, assume you are writing an appellate brief for a judge. Would a judge find my brief easy to read and understand? Would a judge be convinced by my arguments? How will the opposing attorney argue the case? Can I counter his arguments? Respond to his criticism of my arguments?

A final way to develop metacognitive skills is to think how you would teach a concept or skill? How would I explain eminent domain to a first-year student? How would I teach a first-year student to organize an objective memo? How would I teach a first-year student to read and analyze a case?

In sum, developing metacognitive skills is vital to becoming an effective learners. As a group of scholars has argued, "students without metacognitive approaches are essentially students without direction and ability to review their progress, accomplishments, and future learning directions."[62]

Exercise

At the end of your first semester, but before you get your grades, evaluate how you have done. Did you use the best learning techniques? Predict your grades in each class. When you get your grades, see if your predictions were accurate. If not, why not?

Notes

1. Cheryl P. Preston et.al., *Teaching Thinking Like a Lawyer: Metacognition and Law Students*, 2014 BYU L. REV. 1053, 1054 (2015). HTTP:// DIGITALCOMMONS.LAW.BYU.EDU/CGI/VIEWCONTENT.CGI?ARTICLE=2944&CONTEXT=LAWREVIEW

2. *Id.* at 1054.

3. WILLIAM M. SULLIVAN, ANNE COLBY, JUDITH WELCH WEGNER, LLOYD BOND, & LEE S. SHULMAN, EDUCATING LAWYERS: PREPARATION FOR THE PROFESSION OF LAW 217 (Jossey-Bass 2007).

4. Paul G. Middlebrooks et. al., *Studying Metacognitive Processes at the Single Neuron Level*, http://sites.duke.edu/sommerlab/files/2013/09/MiddlebrooksEtAl.pdf at 2 (2014); Michael Hunter Schwartz, *Teaching Law by Design: How Learning Theory and Instructional Design Can Inform and Reform Law Teaching*, 38 SAN DIEGO L. REV. 347, 376 (2001) [hereinafter Schwartz, *Law Teaching*].

5. Cem Balcikanli, *Metacognitive Awareness Inventory for Teachers (MAIT)*, 9 Elec. J. Res. Educ. Psych. 1309, 1312 (2011). [http://www.investigacion-psicopedagogica.org/revista/articulos/25/english/Art_25_563.pdf]

6. Anthony Niedwiecki, *Lawyers and Learning: A Metacognitive Approach to Legal Education*, 13 WIDENER L. REV. 33, 42-43 (2006).

7. Teaching Excellence in Adult Literacy, JUST WRITE GUIDE, https://teal.ed.gov/resources at 41 (2012).

8. *Id.* at 32.

9. Anastasia Efklides, *The Role of Metacognitive Experiences in the Learning Process*, 21 Psicothema 76, 77 (2009). [http://www.unioviedo.es/reunido/index.php/PST/article/download/8799/8663].

10. Metacognitive control is "any instance of cognitive control that is informed by metacognitive knowledge or monitoring." Michael J. Serra & Janet Metcalfe, *Effective Implementation of Metacognition, in* HANDBOOK OF METACOGNITION 270 (Douglas J. Hacker et.al. eds., 2009).

11. Balcikanli, *supra* at 1313-14.

12. JUST WRITE GUIDE, *supra* at 30.

13. Serra & Metcalfe, *supra* at 278.

14. Efklides, *supra* at 78; *see also* Balcikanli, *supra* at 1317 ("Declarative knowledge includes individuals' conceptions, and also their beliefs of task structures, their cognitive goals, and their own abilities.").

15. John H. Flavell, *Metacognition and Cognitive Monitoring: A New Area of Cognitive Development Inquiry*, 34 AM. PSYCH. 906, 907 (1979). [http://www4.ncsu.edu/~jlnietfe/Metacog_Articles_files/Flavell%20%281979%29.pdf].

16. *Id.*

17. Paul R. Pintrich, The Role of Metacognitive Knowledge in Learning, Teaching, and Assessing, 41 THEORY INTO PRACTICE 219, 221 (2002). [http://cursa.ihmc.us/rid=1JTPTQ9XB-1142BSK-17N3/A01-004.pdf]

18. *Id.* at 221-22.

19. Flavell, *supra* at 907.

20. Pintrich, *supra* at 222. On the other hand, "if a person does not believe that he or she can learn, he or she won't." Alice Y. Kolb & David A. Kolb, *The Learning Way: Meta-Cognitive Aspects of Experiential Learning*, 40 SIMULATION GAMING 297, 304 (2009). [http://www.coulthard.com/library/Files/kolbkolb_2009_thelearningway.pdf].

21. Duane F. SHELL ET.AL., THE UNIFIED LEARNING MODEL: HOW MOTIVATIONAL, COGNITIVE, AND NEUROLOGICAL SCIENCES INFORM BEST TEACHING PRACTICES 75 (2010).

22. Marcel V.J. Veenman et.al, *Metacognition and Learning: Conceptual and Methodological Considerations*, 1 METACOGNITION LEARNING 4, 4 (2006). [http://www.csuchico.edu/~nschwartz/Veenman%20Metacognition.pdf] at 4. According to one group of researchers, "[s]tudents' metacognition can be mislead by folk wisdom of a culture about cognition and their making incorrect analyses of their personal mental experiences. The vast majority of adults are not good at planning, selecting, monitoring, and evaluating their strategies of self-regulated learning." University of Memphis, Department of Psychology, *Lifelong Learning at Work and at Home: 25 Learning Principles to Guide Pedagogy and the Design of Learning Environments*, http://psyc.memphis.edu/learning/whatweknow/25principles.doc, at 11 (2008).

23. For heuristics that affect metacognition, see Serra & Metcalfe, *supra* at 281-85. *See also generally* DANIEL KAHNEMAN, THINKING, FAST AND SLOW (2011).

24. Balcikanli, *supra* at 1317; SHELL, *supra* at 39.

25. Pintrich, *supra* at 220. "Cognitive strategies are invoked to *make* cognitive progress, metacognitive strategies to *monitor* it." Flavell, *supra* at 909. In other words, metacognitive strategies concern the thinking process, while cognitive strategies solve detailed problems (a general reading strategy versus using a specific mathematical formula to solve a math problem).

26. Leah M. Christensen, *Legal Reading and Success in Law School: An Empirical Study*, 30 SEATTLE U. L. REV. 603, 608 (2007); *see also* SHELL, *supra* at 45 ("We want students to develop chains of action in response to certain states of the world (conditions) that move through alternative outcomes to acceptable results."); Francisco Cano, *An In-Depth Analysis of the Learning and Study Strategies Inventory (LASSI)*, 66 EDUC. PYSCH. MEAS. 1023, 1023 (2006) (Learning strategies are "any thoughts, behaviors, beliefs or emotions that facilitate the acquisition, understanding or later transfer of new knowledge and skills.").

27. Flavell, *supra* at 907.

28. Pintrich, *supra* at 219-20.

29. *Id.* at 219.

30. *Id.* at 220.

31. Julian Roelle et.al., *The Use of Solved Example Problems for Fostering Strategies of Self-Regulated Learning in Journal Writing*, 2012 Education Research International 1. [http://downloads.hindawi.com/journals/edu/2012/751625.pdf]

32. Pintrich, *supra* at 220.

33. *Id.* at 221.

34. Balcikanli, *supra* at 1317; Pintrich, *supra* at 221.

35. Balcikanli, *supra* at 1317. See also Neil J. Anderson, *The Role of Metacognition in Second Language Teaching and Learning*, http://files.eric.ed.gov/fulltext/ED463659.pdf at 4 ("Knowing how to orchestrate the use of more than one strategy is an important metacognitive skill. The ability to coordinate, organize, and make associations among the various strategies available is a major distinction between strong and weak second language learners.").

36. Pintrich, *supra* at 221.

37. Cindy E. Hmelo-Silver, *Problem-Based Learning: What and How Do Students Learn?*, 16 Educ. Psych. Rev. 235, 240 (2004).

38. Memphis, *supra* at 10.

39. Efklides, *supra* at 79.

40. Balcikanli, *supra* at 1318; *see also* Efklides, *supra* at 80.

41. Efklides, *supra* at 80.

42. Balcikanli, *supra* at 1318.

43. *Id.*

44. *Id.*; *see also* Serra & Metcalfe, *supra* at 279 ("Metacognitive monitoring focuses on the progress of the cognitive process in which the person is engaged.").

45. Jennifer Wiley et. al., *Putting the Comprehension in Metacomprehension*, 132 J. GEN. PYSCH. 408, 408 (2005). [http://scholarworks.boisestate.edu/cgi/viewcontent.cgi?article=1006&context=cifs_facpubs]; *see also* Anderson, *supra* at 3 ("By

monitoring their use of learning strategies, students are better able to keep themselves on track to meet their learning goals."); Michael Hunter Schwartz, *Teaching Law Students to Be Self-Regulated Learners*, 2003 MICH ST. DCL L. REV. 447, 460 [hereinafter Schwartz, *Self-Regulated Learners*].

46. Flavell, *supra* at 909.

47. Wiley, *supra* at 408.

48. Balcikanli, *supra* at 1318.

49. Niedwiecki, *supra* at 62.

50. Schwartz, *Self-Regulated Learners*, *supra* at 460-61.

51. *Id.* at 461.

52. Efklides, *supra* at 77.

53. *Id.*

54. *Id.*

55. *Id.*

56. *Id.* at 81.

57. *Id.*

58. *Id.* at 77.

59. Kolb & Kolb, *supra* at 309.

60. *Id.*

61. *Id.*

62. J. MICHAEL O'MALLEY & ANNA UHL CHAMOT, LEARNING STRATEGIES IN SECOND LANGUAGE ACQUISTION 8 (1990).

Chapter Five
How to Become a Self-Regulated Learner

Chapter Goals.

1. To introduce self-regulated learning.
2. To show you how to become an engaged learner, rather than a lazy one.
3. To teach you the basics of self-regulated learning.
4. To show you the three stages of self-regulated learning: the forethought stage, the performance stage, and the reflective stage.
5. To teach you specific techniques for self-regulated learning, including deliberate practice, focused practice, developing schemas or frameworks (mental models), domain transfer, asking self-regulation questions, and creativity.
6. To teach you how to develop problem-solving skills.

The most important thing you can do to succeed in law school, and in life, is to become a self-regulated (self-directed) learner.[1] Not only will you take charge of your learning, but you will be able to deal with changes in knowledge and skills in the future. The law is constantly changing, and no one can predicted what the law will look like in ten or twenty years.

Few students come to law school as self-regulated learners. Most students consider learning as something that happens to them through lectures and superficial readings.[2] (Has this been your attitude toward learning?) Passive observers do not make effective learners. The human mind is not a sponge.[3] Take charge of your learning!

Similarly, many students come to law school thinking that assignments are something to get through. They often treat assignments like busy work. This is wrong: Law professors give assignments for a reason. However, "[i]nexperienced students see assignments as something to be done; experienced students see them as something to be used. Look on every assignment as a clue from the teacher–what he or she considers important enough to spend time learning. Assignments, in most cases, are solid, meaty chunks of what's important. Don't just do assignments with minimal effort and thought, use them to learn something new."[4]

Finally, students need to understand that they can do things with their learning. Students need to realize that "they are not only discoverers of knowledge but have the capacity themselves to produce knowledge."[5] In particular, being a lawyer is producing knowledge. It is making new arguments and changing the law. It is applying old arguments to new situations. It is using knowledge and skills to help people.

As will become obvious as you read through this chapter, I have already started you on the road to becoming a self-regulated learner, such as in the chapter on study habits and the one on metacognition.

In sum, most people can develop self-regulated learning.[6] It has little to do with IQ, but instead, it depends on self-control, self-discipline, perseverance, determination, avoiding procrastination, and the ability to delay self-gratification.[7] As Professor Max has stated, "Exceptional learning is the process of laying an intellectual framework upon which a student can then build a lifetime of self-direct[ed] learning and exploration. This framework includes the tools for that learning (self-awareness, skepticism, inquisitiveness) as well as motivation to develop that learning (passion, relevance, determination)."[8]

I. Become an Engaged Learner.

<u>Self-regulated learners are engaged learners</u>, and <u>they are fascinated by learning new things</u>. As one scholar has stated, "[i]t is virtually impossible to become proficient at a mental task without extended practice."[9] Think about you favorite athletes. They worked for years to develop their abilities. Everyday for hours a day. They were dedicated to their goal. And, they didn't stop when they achieved mastery. They still train every day to better their craft.

Daniel Kahneman has developed the idea of the 'engaged' thinker.[10] He writes, "[t]hose who avoid the sin of intellectual sloth could be called 'engaged.' They are more alert, more intellectually active, less willing to be satisfied with superficially attractive answers, more skeptical about their intuitions."[11] In contrast, lazy thinkers are characterized by "a reluctance to invest more effort than is strictly necessary."[12] (Engaged thinkers succeed; lazy thinkers fail. Got it.)

Professor Kahneman's idea of engaged and lazy thinkers is based on his concept of how the human mind works. He believes that evolution produced two interactive modes of thinking:

> System 1 operates automatically and quickly, with little or no effort and no sense of voluntary control.

> System 2 allocates attention to the effortful mental activities
> that demand it, including complex computations. The oper-
> ations of System 2 are often associated with the subjective
> experience of agency, choice, and concentration.[13]

Thus, System 1 is unconscious, intuitive thought (automatic pilot), while slower System 2 is conscious, rational thinking (effortful system). The reason that many thinkers are lazy is that cognitive thought in System 2 requires a great deal of mental effort, and people who are unmotivated do not expend that mental effort.[14] In such a situation, lazy thinkers often adopt "a superficially plausible answer that comes readily to mind," which comes from System 1 (which is subject to biases), rather than the correct answer that requires more work.[15] Similarly, "[i]t is important to separate the disposition or willingness to think critically from the ability to think critically. Some people may have excellent critical-thinking skills and may recognize when the skills are needed, but they also may choose not to engage in the effortful process of using them. This is the distinction between what people can do and what they actually do in real-world contexts."[16]

Accordingly, to be an engaged learner, you must have the discipline to overcome the lazy thinking of System 2 and the biases of System 1. As Kahneman has declared, "[e]ven in the absence of time pressure, maintaining a coherent train of thought requires discipline."[17] (I need to be a disciplined learner. Got it.)

One reason that you must be an engaged learner is that it takes many years of intense training to develop expertise, such as to be a lawyer.[18] Expertise requires a powerful memory.[19] "The acquisition of expertise in complex tasks such as high-level chess, professional basketball, or firefighting is intricate and slow because expertise in a domain is not a single skill but rather a large collection of miniskills."[20] Kahneman estimates that it takes 10,000 hours of practice to become a chess master.[21] Similarly, *Best Practices* has noted concerning legal education, "Developing problem-solving expertise requires repetitions of 'training' as against the hard world of consequences, of repeated success and failure, and some inductive efforts at understanding what works and what does not, what seems important and what does not."[22]

Engaged learners put forth the effort to master their field. They understand that success in a domain "requires extensive factual knowledge."[23] Trying to learn skills, such as analysis or synthesis, in the absence of factual knowledge is impossible."[24] Likewise, context is essential for understanding.[25] In addition, "memory is the cognitive process of *first* resort. When faced with a problem, you will first search for a solution in memory, and if you find one, you will very likely use it."[26] The cognitive process of second resort is analogy–comparing problems to ones stored in long-term memory.[27] (This means that relying on an outside sources, such as Wikipedia, should be a last resort.) Those who succeed in a field, such as chess masters, have the best long-term memories, and such experts "can access the information from memory with great speed and accuracy."[28] (Do you think a chess master looks up moves in the middle of a match? Do you think a violinist looks up a fingering technique in the middle of a concert?) However, researchers have demonstrated that "average people can achieve extraordinary memory ability by developing their own retrieval structures or being given them by researchers."[29]

Being an engaged learner requires more than effort (being behaviorally engaged); you must also be cognitively engaged.[30] "In this sense, cognitive engagement refers to the quality of students' engagement, whereas sheer effort refers to the quantity of their engagement in the class. This outcome of cognitive engagement is the most important one for understanding classroom learning. . ."[31] Cognitive engagement requires preparation for learning, goal setting, attention, focus, self-monitoring, and reflection. (I give the details below.)

Self-engaged learners don't stop when the learning is difficult because they have a growth mindset.[32] If they don't understand a case on first reading, they read it as many time as necessary to fully understand it. Self-engaged learners don't stop when their first strategy fails; they try another approach. Self-engaged learners welcome challenges. They seek feedback, and they accept criticism because it helps them improve. Self-engaged learners do more than the professor requires because it is the acquisition of knowledge and skills that is important, not just getting good grades.

Obviously, developing a growth mindset, as discussed in Chapter One, is an important step in becoming an engaged learner. With a growth mindset, you focus on the implications for learning, rather than about judging yourself.[33] You welcome mistakes. You develop curiosity and a love for knowledge.[34]

Exercises

1. Is the law static, or does it change?
2. If it changes, do you need a different skill set than if it is passive? How?
3. Are you a passive learner? Do you think that learning is something that

happens to you? What is the effect of being a passive learner?

4. Do you think you can produce knowledge? When a lawyer handles a case, is the lawyer producing new knowledge? How? Reflect on these questions.

5. When you receive an assignment, do you just put in minimal effort? If yes, how does this affect your learning? Your grades?

6. Are you an engaged learner? If not, do you think that this affected your grades in college?

7. What is intellectual sloth? Do you want to be a sloth?

8. What are System 1 and System 2? How does System 1 hurt learning?

9. How long does it take to develop expertise? Do you want to be an expert attorney?

10. Why is factual knowledge important for learning?

11. What is cognitively engaged? Are you cognitively engaged when you study?

12. On a scale of 1-10, rate your cognitive engagement in college? In class? When studying? When writing papers? When doing projects?

13. Think of one college class you liked? Were you cognitively engaged in that class? Why? Did you learn more in that class? Did you get a good grade in that class?

14. What is your attitude to making mistakes? What is your attitude to doing difficult tasks?

15. Do you have curiosity and a love of knowledge? Can you develop curiosity and love of knowledge for the law? (If you do, it will make your life a lot easier.)

II. The Basics of Self-Regulated Learning.

A law professor has given an excellent summary of self-regulation: "setting a goal, taking steps to try to achieve that goal, assessing the impact of effort, . . . determining how to improve that impact, and taking responsive action."[35] (Can you see how this is a process?) This section will focus on the basics of self-regulated learning, and the following section will give you specific self-regulation techniques.

First, self-regulation requires self-control. As one writer has declared, "Self-control is important to achieving goals."[36] She continued, "Self-control is the capacity to decide what to do and when, and to forgo temptation and delay reward. Willpower amounts to the application of limited cognitive resources, such as devising a list of options, crafting a plan, and making a decision – it is energy gets depleted with use. Willpower is not exercised, it is self-control that we expend."[37]

Obviously, <u>self-control involves emotional control</u>.[38] "[T]he successful learner internalizes his locus of control, and feels empowered to attribute success and failures to his own study habits and efforts."[39] (Again, you've seen this before.) Self-regulated learning has a strong positive affect on self-efficacy, which, in turn, increases motivation. (see Chapter One)

Self- regulated learning also requires 1) strategic knowledge, 2) knowledge about cognitive tasks, and 3) self-knowledge.

> 1) <u>Strategic knowledge</u> "encompasses knowledge of . . . different types of learning strategies and heuristics for different types of tasks; knowing the steps and algorithms needed for solving problems and recurring technical tasks, the need to plan, monitor, and evaluate [] learning and thinking; and effective strategies for rehearsal (memorizing), elaboration (using learning devices such as summarizing, paraphrasing, and linking new knowledge to private knowledge, and organization of the material" (concept maps).[40]
>
> 2) <u>Knowledge about cognitive tasks</u> "includes comprehending the directions (such as knowing what the verbs mean), assessing the difficulty of the task, and deciding wisely which learning and thinking strategies to use."[41]
>
> 3) <u>Self-knowledge</u> "entails knowing one's strengths and weakness as a learner, accurately judging one's command of the material and knowing what strategies work best for oneself to accomplish given tasks.[42]

One might note that many of the above details overlap with metacognition. <u>Metacognition is a key part of self-regulated learning</u>.[43] "Metacognition involves feedback on one's learning," while "self-regulation encompasses the monitoring and managing of one's cognitive processes as well as the awareness of and control over one's emotions, behavior, and environment as related to learning."[44] (Are you starting to see how everything I am talking about in this book fits together?)

Exercises

1. What is self-control? Do you have self-control over your learning?

2. How is emotional control involved in self-regulated learning?
3. Do you have emotional control over your learning? Have you ever struggled with learning because of your emotions? Think carefully about this last question?
4. What are the three requirements of self-regulated learning? Why are each of these requirements important?
5. How is metacognition a part of self-regulated learning?

A legal educator has divided self-regulated learning for specific tasks into three parts: forethought, performance, and reflection, then subdivided each of the parts.[45] Notice that I already introduced this model when I modified it for the critical reasoning section. (Got it; three parts: before, during, after.)

The forethought stage involves the thought processes you undertake before you start the learning (or reading or problem-solving) task–"task perception, self-efficacy, self-motivation, goal setting, and strategic planning."[46] In the task stage, you should perceive and react to the task.[47] First, you should identify and classify the task, by perceiving its skill domain and the subject of the task.[48] For law learning, the skill domain will be a legal subject, and the subject of the task is learning that particular subject. For example, the task may concern learning the types of homicide in Criminal Law. In addition, in the task stage, you should react to the task, by determining how much the learning interests you, establishing relevance to learning goals, and relating the task to prior knowledge.[49] (He keeps talking about relating new material to prior knowledge. This must be important for learning.)

In the second forethought substage, you "assesses [your] efficacy for accomplishing the task."[50] (I also mentioned self-efficacy in connection with motivation in Chapter One). Self-efficacy involves four factors: "(1) [your] current skill level, (2) the extent to which you have witnessed modeling from peers and teachers. . ., (3) verbal persuasion regarding the difficulty of the task, and (4) [your] current psychological state."[51] You should know your skill and experience levels. Having a positive attitude and confidence in yourself makes you a better learner.[52]

Self-motivation is a key to being a self-regulated learner. A learner who wants to learn is more motivated than a learner who learns something just to earn a good grade. As I mentioned in Chapter One, setting goals is fundamental to motivation.[53] Other ways to help self-motivation include replacing negative self-talk (usually from prior experiences) with "positive self-instruction and a sense of self as an effective [learner]" and developing new habits.[54] Developing metacognitive strategies (ways to monitor one's thinking; Chapter Four) also helps motivation because using them builds confidence.[55]

Based on the earlier stages, you then set goals (purposes) for the learning (the desired outcome).[56] Remember that I said in Chapter One that having learning goals for a task was better than having other types of goals. It is often good to have a real world purpose when learning.[57] Why are you doing this assignment and what do you want to accomplish? In coming up with a purpose, you should be as specific as possible. "The purpose of this task is to learn personal jurisdiction through three cases and supplementary material. By the end of the class, I want to be able to synthesize the law of personal jurisdiction and apply it to real world problems."

Similarly, you must consider the context of the learning task. For example, how does learning personal jurisdiction relate to your goals in Civil Procedure? How does this task relate to other subjects you have learned? How does this task relate to what lawyers do?

The final step in the forethought stage is developing a learning (or reading or problem-solving; this applies to everything) strategy based on the earlier substages.[58] Strategies are "set[s] of mental processes" used by a thinker to achieve a purpose.[59] "The best performers make the most specific technique-oriented plans."[60] In other words, strategies are ways to achieve your purpose. You should think about the steps you will take in learning material and the tools you will use. It might help to write down your learning strategy for a task to help you form better strategies.

The performance stage is the actual learning (or reading or problem-solving). This stage encompasses three processes: (1) "attention-focusing," (2) "the activity itself," and (3) "the self-monitoring [you] performs as [you] implement [your] strategies and start to learn."[61] Attention-focusing helps make the learning productive. Self-regulated learners are able to focus their attention.[62] Having a purpose or goal when learning helps attention-focusing, as does being enthusiastic about learning. (He keeps mentioning motivation, enthusiasm, and curiosity. They must be important.) An effective learner self-monitors while learning. Make sure you have a checklist in your head of what you what to look for when self-monitoring. In fact, you might want to write this down the first few times you self-monitor. Things to look for: Am I devoting full attention to my learning? Do I understand what I am learning? If not, what shall I do (re-read, do outside reading, etc.)? Am I being efficient in my learning? Am I remembering what I am learning? Can I connect this learning with prior knowledge? Can I organize this learning into a schema?

The activity substage is the actual learning. I have lots on this substage throughout this book, such as Chapter Two on study habits.

The final stage is the reflective (or evaluation) stage. (He keeps mentioning reflection. This must be important, too.) In this stage, the learner critically reflects on what she learned (or read or the problem solved) and how effectively she did it.[63] The reflective stage is very important in helping you improve your learning and efficiency. Did you accomplish your goals in the learning? Did you fully understand the concepts? Did it take longer to learn the concepts than it should have (efficiency)? If so, why? Did you have enough context (background) before started? What did you get from task? Did you relate the learning to your prior knowledge? How did you feel about how you performed the task? Did you learn something about your learning methods? (Learning is an endless circle.)

Exercises

1. What are the three-stages of self-regulated learning? Do you regularly use each stage when you do a learning task?
2. What is the forethought stage? Describe each substep of the forethought stage. Why are each of these substeps important? Which of these substeps do you currently use in your learning?
3. Do you have a learning strategy when you want to learn something?
4. What is the performance stage? Describe the substeps of the performance stage? Why is each substep important? Why is self-monitoring particularly important?
5. What is the reflective stage? Why is it important? Do you usually reflect on what you have learned after you do the learning? Do you usually evaluate the effectiveness of your learning process after you have finished your learning? Can you see why this could help your learning?

III. Specific Techniques for Self-Regulated Learning

Many of the learning techniques I have already discussed in this book, such as self-testing, reflection, and self-evaluation, are important parts of being a self-regulated learner.[64] Here are some additional techniques.

Deliberate practice is a key skill for self-regulated learners. There are two types of practice (such as learning material): practice to automaticity and deliberate practice.[65] With the usual type, the learner works at a skill to reach automaticity, after which the skill can be executed with little effort.[66] On the other hand, the <u>intense concentration</u> required for deliberate practice distinguishes it from the other type.[67] "Individuals engaged in deliberate practice tend to resist automaticity," and they "strive to continuously achieve mastery of increasingly higher levels of performance through the acquisition of more complex and refined cognitive mechanisms."[68] Deliberate learners focus on the "not yet attained and challenging tasks beyond their current level of performance. . ."[69] <u>They break practice into steps,</u> and they monitor their practice to identify and correct errors.[70] Deliberate practice is not easy, and it often results in failure.[71] "Individuals are motivated to practice because practice improves performance."[72] In other words, engaged learners use deliberate practice to improve their engagement; they challenge themselves. As two professors have argued, "only through deliberate practice, that process of doing, erring, feedback, and incorporating that feedback into subsequent efforts, will students become better learners, stronger performers, and, ultimately, experts in the field."[73]

<u>Focused practice, adopting focused strategies for learning, is part of deliberate practice.</u>[74] Focused practice involves specificity, rather than just performing an action several times.[75] It "involves repeating a specific strategy with the attention to improving detailed aspects of the strategy."[76] It "presents performers with tasks that are initially outside their realm of reliable performance, yet can be mastered within hours of practice by concentrating on critical aspects and by gradually refining performance after feedback."[77] (Do you think that the performers described in the previous sentence have fixed or growth mindsets?)

Here are <u>the elements of deliberative practice</u>: First, it must be designed to specifically improve performance.[78] Second, deliberate practice requires repetition.[79] Third, feedback must be continuously available.[80] Fourth, the practice must be highly demanding mentally.[81] Finally, deliberate practice isn't fun.[82]

Here is an example: A violinist wants to perfect a phrase in a Brahms' sonata. (Begin formative stage) First, she determines how the phrase fits with neighboring phrases. Next, she exams the details of the phrase itself, including looking at all the composer's notations and finding the high point of the phrase. She then determines the direction of the phrase. (E.g., get gradually louder until the first note of the third measure, then get gradually softer.) (Begin performance stage.) Then, she practices the phrase over and over until she can play exactly how she thought it out. Of course, she self-monitors her performance, and gives her full attention to the performance.)

(Begin reflective stage). Afterwards, she thinks about her interpretation and performance again to make certain that she played the phrase as best as she could (reflection and evaluation).

Chess masters, golfers, and . . . successful law students use a similar type of deliberative practice when they are practicing or studying.

Deliberate practice helps learners develop schemas or frameworks (ways to store knowledge in chunks) to organize knowledge.[83] (You can compare a schema to a spice rack where everything is in the right place, so that you can easily retrieve it.) (Do you watch *Sherlock*? In that series, Sherlock Holmes uses a mind-palace, which is like a schema.) From a neurobiological viewpoint, such practice "causes [experts'] brains to develop better systems for storing, organizing, and accessing information in their area of expertise."[84] (Remember, knowledge is stored in neurons, which are interconnected by synapses. These interconnected neurons are chunks.) "A mental model [schemas] not only enables remarkable recall, it helps top performers understand new information better than average performers, since they see it not as an isolated bit of data but as part of a large and com-prehensible picture."[85] Stated differently, "When experts retrieve information, experts retrieve an entire integrated network of existing, interconnected in-formation built over multiple retrieval and consolidation cycles spaced over years."[86]

(Before going on, reflect for a few minutes on how you can use deliberate practice in your learning.)

Effective learners use mental models to help distinguish relevant from irrelevant information.[87] (I have noticed that struggling law students often have difficulty distinguishing relevant from irrelevant information.) Effective learners also employ mental models to "project what will happen next."[88] In sum, "Since a mental model is understanding of how your domain functions as a system, you know how changes in the system's inputs will affect the outputs–that is how the events that just happened will create events that are about to happen."[89]

Here is how the mind creates schemas through chunking. When two sensory inputs are in working (or short-term) memory together then stored in long-term memory, the two inputs will form a neural pattern (a chunk). When one of inputs is retrieved, it fires the neuron of the other one because the neurons are chained together by synapses (matching).[90] This function also occurs when more than two inputs are involved in the pattern.[91] The fact that this can continue infinitely "is how our knowledge of things and concepts are built."[92]

In other words, "One small chunk at a time, you link the pieces together in a pattern that your brain can access."[93] For example, human brains store the appearance, taste, and odor of an apple together.[94] Consequently, when a person sees an apple, she can also link to its smell and taste.[95]

In sum, creating schemas is about creating connections. Connections organize knowledge.[96] Experts have many connections between nodes, while novices have few connections.[97] As a law student you need to create many connections between related knowledge.

(Before you go on, reflect for a few minutes on the importance of schemas and how you can organize knowledge.)

Self-regulated learners develop the habit of employing their skills across domains (domain transfer). Stated simply: domain transfer is applying existing skills to a new situation; it is an analogical skill.[98] "When critical-thinking skills are taught so that they transfer appropriately and spontaneously, students learn to actively focus on the structure of problems or arguments so the underlying characteristics become salient, instead of the domain-specific surface characteristics."[99] The key to this process "involves the ability of external cues to trigger retrieval processes in long-term memory, so information about a thinking skill can move into working memory, where it can be consciously considered."[100] This hinges upon how the skill was originally learned, how information is stored in long term-memory, and how it was used.[101] "Information that is associated with material being learned can function as an effective retrieval cue when the learning is completed."[102]

Transfer involves schemas. As noted above, one can effectively organize material in long-term memory by developing "interconnected knowledge structures" (schemas)–relating concepts to other concepts.[103] In other words, "the brain has a formal way of organizing interconnected ideas, and a precondition to mastery of the material is understanding the hierarchy, order, and organization – or schema – of that material."[104] As one legal educator has written, "The more schemas a person has available for comparison, the better a pervasive schematic can illuminate the differences between patterns in situations, training the brain to search for knowledge that can be generalized and applied to solve a new problem. Therefore, because human beings tie their learning to very specific patterns, any solution to the transfer problem in law school must involve the search for highly inclusive meta-schematics that can span multiple contexts, as well as stimulate students to access those cognitive maps through learner motivation and metacognitive strategies."[105]   The following cognitive areas are transferable: knowledge (substantive law), skills, concepts, attitudes, principles, and dispositions.[106]

As you can see, domain transfer is a vital learning and thinking skill. Those who lack domain transfer ability are limited in what they can do. (How were your domain transfer skills in college?) Domain transfer is especially important for lawyers because they generally have to deal with so many fields, including non-legal ones, such as handling medical malpractice cases, which involves medical knowledge. Domain transfer also helps law students because it helps them get the big picture earlier. Instead of dealing with every subject area as separate from the others.

One professor has used sunk costs–"The general idea . . . that prior investments are not relevant to decisions about future costs"–as an example.[107] She writes, "The goal of transferable thinking skills would be achieved if students recognize sunk-costs arguments when they are being made in totally different settings and can apply what has been learned about these arguments in the new settings."[108] Her first example of a sunk cost is a friend who is investing $500 to repair a beat-up, old car, which he has already "sunk" a lot of money into. Under the sunk-cost theory, the previous investment is irrelevant. A creative thinker would then be able to transfer sunk-cost concepts to dissimilar situations, such as Congress spending additional money on a defective missile system, which it has already spent millions on, or a man marrying a girlfriend because they have already spent so much time together.

Examples of domain transfer in the law would be transferring concepts of fairness from tort law to contracts law or transferring concepts of federalism to choice of law. The transfer could also be transferring a method of solving a property problem to a contracts problem. Likewise, applying principles from statutes and cases to drafting contracts is transfer.[109] Finally, using a teaching technique from one area in another area is transfer.

Working with errors is also an important self-regulation learning technique. Self-regulated students are not afraid of making errors because they learn from errors. Look for errors in your work, and correct them.

You can also develop your self-regulated learning skills by asking yourself self-regulated questions (which look a lot like metacognitive questions.) For example, at the end of a reading, you could ask yourself "what were the five most important things in the reading?" Similarly, after a class, ask "what were the five most important things the professor talked about today?" Or, after the end of the semester, ask yourself: "how have I improved my learning skills this semester? How can I improve them more?"

Finally, creativity is also part of the self-regulation process. A twenty-first century worker must be "someone who can carry out multistep operations, manipulate abstract and complex symbols and ideas, efficiently acquire new information, and remain flexible enough to recognize the need for continuing change and new paradigms for lifelong learning."[110] In college, I was taught a two-step approach to creativity. First, "brainstorm" to come up with as many ideas as possible with out being critical in any way. Second, criticize the results. For example, think about as many uses for a clothes line as possible, then discuss which of these uses are practical and useful.

Another form of creative thinking is lateral thinking–thinking outside the box.[111] The creative thinker sees things no one else sees. He steps outside the confines of logic (logic can only take us so far) and the protocols of a field to find a better answer. He is not stopped by the difficulty of a problem, nor the fact that others say it can't be done.

You can also improve your self-regulation in class. First, you should be fully prepared to listen (critical listening) and participate in class. You should write out questions during the assigned reading. Second, you should self-engage in class. You should determine what are the most important points. You should connect the new information with what you already know. You should mentally challenge what is being said. You should consider the implications about what is being said. You should ask and answer questions. You should participate in class exercises. Third, as I've mentioned before, you should review the class shortly after the class, self-test and reflect on the class. Finally, you should be constantly asking yourself "how could I have prepared better for class?", how could I have absorbed the lecture better?", "how could I have participated in the class better?", etc.

Exercises

1. What is deliberate practice? Why is it an important part of self-regulated learning?
2. What is focused practice?
3. What are the steps of deliberate practice?
4. Have you used deliberate practice in the past? College? Sports? Music? Think how you can use deliberate practice in your learning.
5. What is a schema? Why are schemas important for learning?
6. How does chunking create schemas? Why are connections important? Who has more connections? Experts or novices?
7. What is domain transfer? Why is it important? Why is it important for lawyers?

8. How does a student develop domain transfer skills?

9. Give other examples of sunk costs.

10. Why is working with errors helpful?

11. What are self-regulated questions? Write out several self-regulated questions for your learning.

12. Are you creative? If not, can you become creative? (If you said no, stop and re-read the section on the growth mindset.) What are some creativity techniques? Practice them.

13. How can you improve your self-regulation in class?

IV. Problem-Solving

It is important for self-regulated learners to be problem-solvers. They must have several problem-solving approaches, and they must know when to use a particular one. (What type of metacognitive knowledge is the second half of this sentence involve?)

The goal of law school is to develop legal problem-solvers. For example, litigators solve problems for clients. A client who has been "wronged" will bring that problem to an attorney for a legal solution. For instance, your client may have entered into a contract to sell 50,000 widgets to another party at $5 per widget. When the time for delivery arrived, the other party refused delivery and refused to pay. The client wants you to solve this problem. First, you will probably negotiate with the other party, and if that fails, you will file a lawsuit (after having researched the law and the facts).

Similarly, your client may have been involved in an automobile accident, which he thinks was the other driver's fault. Your client suffered $500,00 damages for hospital bills and $15,000 damages to his car. You will probably start by talking to the opposing party's insurance company. You will also need to determine whether your state's no-fault law applies. If all else fails and you think you have a good case, you will probably file suit.

Of course, your client may be the defendant in a case similar to the ones above. In that case, the problem you are solving is to make sure your client doesn't have to pay damages or, at least to smaller damages than was sued for.

Most law students believe that trying to win is always the goal during litigation. It is not. The best attorneys obtain the best outcome for the client based on the circumstances. Say your client has been sued for five million dollars in a medical malpractice case. You know your client will lose at trial, so, you try to negotiate a settlement with the opposing attorney. The opposing party will not settle for less than five million dollars so you go to trial. At trial the other party prevails, but only gets five hundred thousand dollars in damages because you did a good job limiting damages. Did you do a good job for your client? Of course you did; you saved her 4.5 million. You are a good legal problem-solver.

Here is another example. You client has been sued for fifty thousand dollars for breach of contract. After fully researching the problem, you determine that your client cannot prevail at trial and will have to pay the full fifty thousand. What do you do? Of course, the first thing you try to do is settle, but assume the other side won't settle for less than fifty thousand. The answer: you tell the client to pay the fifty thousand. If you go to trial your client will lose fifty thousand and have to pay an attorney's fee. (Say $10,000 + $50,000=$60,000). Obviously it is better for your client to settle; she will save ten thousand. But wait; don't you lose ten thousand in attorney's fees. Yes, but litigating just so that you can get your fee is unethical. It's also bad strategy. If you get a reputation as a dishonest lawyer, you won't get any attorney's fees at all.

Litigators are not the only legal problem-solvers. When an attorney writes a will for a client, she is solving a problem for her client–how to distribute the client's estate to his loved ones. Drafting a contract is similarly problem-solving. In drafting a contract, an attorney is giving legal force to the parties' agreement.

Let's get to the basics of legal problem-solving. Problem solving is "the ability to combine previously learned principles, procedures, declarative knowledge, and cognitive strategies in a unique way within a domain of content to solve previously unencountered problems."[112] For law, problem solving often "involves identifying and evaluating the analytical arguments reasonable lawyers would make with respect to the particular set of legal issues presented by a fact pattern and then predicting how a court would assess those arguments and resolve each issue."[113] (Keep re-reading these definitions until you have a clear picture of what legal problem-solving is.) (Let's reflect. Unencountered problems. That means a new problem. "The ability to combine previously learned principles, procedures, declarative knowledge, and cognitive strategies in a unique way within a domain of content." So, I want to solve the problem with strategies I know, but I should combine them in a new way based on context–the particular problem. So, problem-solving has to be flexible.) (Now, do the same reflection for the legal problem-solving sentence.)

Most problem-solving strategies will reflect the three stages of self-regulated learning: forethought, performance, reflection. Here is a general problem-solving strategy I like: 1) Identify the problem, 2) Define the problem, 3) Form a strategy, 4) Organize information, 5) Solve the problem (including monitoring your progress), 6) Evaluate the solution.[114] (Which of these steps correspond to the three stages of self-regulated learning?) Of course, the approach you use will depend on the problem. Here is a strategy to solve a legal problem: Gather facts, frame issues, research, analyze cases, synthesis, develop problem-solving strategy, apply law to facts, form conclusions, write up, evaluate.

Let's try the legal strategy with a problem like you might be given in a legal writing class. Your professor has given you a set of facts concerning a client's tort litigation, and he wants you to determine whether you can file suit in State X.

Identify the problem: As you read through the facts, you notice that the defendant has only a few connections with State X. That suggests to you that the issue might be whether a court in State X has personal jurisdiction over the defendant. When you reflect on the problem further, you decide that the issue is personal jurisdiction. Why is this important? If your firm files suit in State X and the court doesn't have personal jurisdiction over the defendant, the court will dismiss the case, and you will have to file the case elsewhere. This will cause a significant delay in your client's case, and he will incur unnecessary attorney's fees. You should also check the facts carefully to see if there is any other material issue you want to research at this time. (Assume there isn't.)

Define the problem: This involves framing the issue. "Does State X have personal jurisdiction over a defendant when that defendant's contacts with State X comprise . . ." After you have stated the issue, make sure that you fully understand everything related to the issue.

Form a strategy: In this case, your strategy will probably be to do research concerning the law of personal jurisdiction as it relates to the facts of your case. If you do not know much about personal jurisdiction you might want to start with background reading, such as the personal jurisdiction chapter in a civil procedure treatise. You then determine your research strategy. Will I use Lexis? A digest? If so which digest? How will I double-check my research? Etc.

Brief cases: After you have found the relevant law, you need to analyze it.

<u>Develop problem-solving strategy</u>: You will want to organize the material, which in this case means synthesizing the law. Then you will apply the synthesized law to the facts.

<u>Synthesize</u>: Form a coherent, consistent rule based on the cases you have found. (Also, see what else you can get out of the cases, such as rule explanation or rule illustration.)

<u>Apply the law to the facts</u>: Do this in detail.

<u>Form conclusions</u>: What is the solution to the problem.

<u>Write it up</u>: You will be taught the various forms of how to write up problems such as objective memoranda and appellate briefs in legal writing.

<u>Evaluate</u>: Have you come up with the best solution based on the law and facts? Are there other possible solutions? Etc.

Of course, the above model is not a rigid model. You can go back to earlier steps, if necessary.

I know that the above model looks daunting on first view. However, here is the point: if you adopt a consistent approach with problem-solving, it will make your job easier. Doing one step at a time is a lot easier than attacking a large problem with no strategy. Using a process applies to everything–problem-solving, studying, doing research, hitting a curve ball, baking a cake.

Exercises

1. Do you have an approach to solving-problems?
2. Can you see why it's important to approach problem-solving as a process?
3. Do you need different problem-solving methods for different problems?
4. Why is winning not always the best approach in litigation?

Important Self-Regulation Techniques

1. Emotional control.
2. Self-Efficacy.
3. Self-Motivation.
4. Self-Awareness.
5. Curiosity.
6. Creativity.
7. Treating learning as a process. (Ex. Forethought stage, performance stage,

evaluative stage, with all the substages.)
8. Self-testing.
9. Monitoring.
10. *Reflection.
11. Self-Evaluation.
12. Deliberate practice.
13. Organizing and remembering through schemas.
14. Domain transfer.
15. Class preparation.
16. Critical listening.
17. Problem-solving.

Exercises

1. How is a self-regulated learner like being a professional athlete? Like a chess master? Like a violinist?
2. Write out the characteristics you possess of a self-regulated learner. Write out the characteristics you don't posses of a self-regulated learner.
3. Can you see why being a self-regulated learner is necessary for being a successful lawyer?
4. Start immediately to develop the above self-regulation techniques. Which one will you try first? Why?

Wrap-Up Question

1. What is the most important thing you need to become a self-regulated learner?[115]

Notes

1. Self-regulated learners are at level 4 of the developmental stages of learning I mentioned in the Preface. They are self-authoring.

2. Robert Leamnson, *Learning (You First Job)*, https://www1.udel.edu/CIS/106/iaydin/07F/misc/firstJob.pdf. at 1.

3. Shailini Jandial George, *Teaching the Smartphone Generation: How Cognitive Science Can Improve Learning in Law School*, 66 MAINE L.REV. 163, 186 (2017).

4. Leamnson, *supra* at 9.

5. MICHAEL HUNTER SCHWARTZ ET.AL., WHAT THE BEST LAW TEACHERS DO 289 (2013) (Robert Corrada).

6. *Creating Self-Regulated Learners: Strategies to Strengthen Students' Self-Awareness and Learning Skills* 4 (2013).

7. *Id.* at 4, 78-79.

8. SCHWARTZ ET.AL., *supra* at 31 (2013) (CRAIG MAX).

9. Daniel T. Willingham, WHY DON'T STUDENTS LIKE SCHOOL: A Cognitive Scientist Answers Questions about How the Mind Works and What it Means for the Classroom 107 (2009); *see also* GEOFF COLVIN, TALENT IS OVERRATED: WHAT REALLY SEPARATES WORLD-CLASS PER-FORMERS FROM EVERYBODY ELSE 60 (2008) ("The results were extraordinarily clear.").

10. DANIEL KAHNEMAN, THINKING, FAST AND SLOW 46 (2011).

11. *Id.* at 46.

12. *Id.* at 31.

13. *Id.* at 20-21.

14. *Id.* at 41-46.

15. *Id.* at 45-46.

16. Diane F. Halpern, *Teaching Critical Thinking for Transfer across Domains: Dispositions, Skills, Structure Training, and Metacognitive Monitoring*, 53 AM. PSYCH. 449, 451 (1998).

17. KAHNEMAN, *supra* at 40.

18. *Id.* at 238; *see also* ROBERT J. MARZANO ET.AL, BECOMING A REFLECTIVE TEACHER 7 (2012); COLVIN, *supra* at 61-2.

19. DUANE F. SHELL ET.AL., THE UNIFIED LEARNING MODEL: HOW MOTIVATIONAL, COGNITIVE, AND NEURO-BIOLOGICAL SCIENCES INFORM BEST TEACHING PRACTICES 09 (2010).

20. KAHNEMAN, *supra* at 238.

21. *Id.*

22. ROY STUCKEY ET AL., BEST PRACTICES IN LEGAL EDUCATION 142 (2007).

23. Willingham, *supra* at 25.

24. *Id.*

25. *Id.* at 121.

26. *Id.* at 37.

27. *Id.* at 40.

28. *Id.* at 39, 131. Do not use a "poor memory" as an excuse for failure. As noted throughout this book, long-term memory is created mainly by effort and the proper approach.

29. DWECK, *supra* note , at 16.

30. Paul R. Pintrich, *Motivation and Classroom Learning, in* 2 HANDBOOK OF PSYCHOLOGY at 105 (2003).

31. *Id.*

32. DWECK, *supra* note , at 53.

33. *Id.* at 209.

34. *Id.* at 53.

35. Heather M. Field, *A Tax Professor's Guide to Formative Assessment*, https:// papers.ssrn.com/sol3/papers.cfm?abstract_id=3388943 at 17 (2019).

36. Debra S. Austin, *Windmills of Your Mind: Understanding the Neurobiology of Emotion*, https://papers.ssrn.com/sol3/papers.cfm?abstract_id=3374006 (2019).

37. *Id.*

38. NILSON,

39. *Id.* at 12.

40. *Id.* at 2-3.

41. *Id.* at 3.

42. *Id.*

43. *Id.* at 5-6.

44. *Id.* at 5.

45. Michael Hunter Schwartz, *Teaching Law Students to be Self-Regulated Learners*, 2003 MICH. ST. DCL L. REV. 447, 454 (2003) [hereinafter Schwartz, *Teaching Law Students*]; *see also* NILSON, *supra* AT 9; COLVIN, *supra* note , at 116-21 (Before the work, during the work, after the work).

46. Schwartz, *Teaching Law Students*, *supra* at 455.

47. *Id.* at 456.

48. *Id.*

49. *Id.*

50. *Id.*; *see also* SHELL, *supra* at 74-76. See Chapter One for a fuller discussion of efficacy.

51. Teaching Excellence in Adult Literacy, JUST WRITE GUIDE, https://teal.ed.gov/resources at 29 (2012).

52. Positive emotions affect self-efficacy. SHELL, *supra* at 75-76.

53. *Id.* at 76.

54. JUST WRITE GUIDE, *supra* at 30.

55. *Id.* at 33.

56. Schwartz, *Teaching Law Students*, *supra* at 457; *see also* COLVIN, *supra* at 116-17 ([T]he poorest performers don't set goals at all; they just slog through their work.").

57. James Stratman posits that students understand more when they read with a "real world purpose" (as a judge, an advocate, etc.), rather than merely preparing for class. James F. Stratman, *When Law Students Read Cases: Exploring Relations between Professional Legal Reasoning Roles and Problem Detection*, 34 DISCOURSE PROCESSES 57 (2002). The same is true for all types of thinking.

58. Schwartz, *Teaching Law Students*, *supra* at 457; Peter Dewitz, *Legal Education: A Problem of Learning from Text*, 23 N.Y.U. L. REV. L. & SOC. CHANGE 225, 228 (1997) (Strategic readers "set a purpose for reading, self-question, search for important information, make inferences, summarize, and monitor the developing meaning."). "Strategies help make explicit the routines and techniques employed by effective learners so that *all* learners can be more effective." JUST WRITE GUIDE, *supra* at 39.

59. *See* Leah M. Christensen, *Legal Reading and Success in Law School: An Empirical Study*, 30 SEATTLE U. L. REV. 603, 608 (2007); *see also* COLVIN, *supra* at 117 ([T]he best performers are focused on how they get better at some specific element of the work, just as a pianist may focus on improving a particular passage.").

60. COLVIN, *supra* at 117.

61. Schwartz, *Teaching Law Students*, *supra* at 458.

62. *Id.* at 458-59.

63. *Id.* at 460-61.

64. Professor Linda B. Nilson has presented countless examples of self-regulated learning exercises in her book *Creating Self-Regulated Learners: Strategies to Strengthen Students' Self-Awareness and Learning Skills* (2013).

65. MARZANO, *supra* at 6-7; SHELL, *supra* at 156-57.

66. MARZANO, *supra* at 6.

67. K. Anders Ericsson, *The Influence of Experience and Deliberate Practice on the Development of Superior Expert Performance*, *in* THE CAMBRIDGE BOOK OF EXPERTISE AND EXPERT PERFORMANCE 694 (K. Anders Ericsson et.al. eds., 2006) [*hereinafter* Ericsson, Deliberate Practice].

68. Marzano, *supra* at 7 (quoting K. Anders Ericsson et. al., *Giftedness and Evidence for Reproducibly Superior Performance: An Account Based on the Expert Performance Framework*, 18 HIGH ABILITY STUDIES 3, 24 (2007) [hereinafter Ericsson, *Expert Performance*]; *see also* COLVIN, *supra* at 63.

69. Ericsson, *Expert Performance*, *supra* at 24; *see also* SHELL, *supra* at 156.

70. NILSON, forward, *supra* at 6 (2013).

71. MARZANO, *supra* at 7.

72. Ericsson, *supra* at 368.

73. Corie Rosen & Hillary Burgess, *More than Merely Doing: Deliberate Practice, Feedback, and Academic Success*, THE LEARNING CURVE 2, 4 (Spring 2010).

74. Marzano, *supra* at 49.

75. *Id.*

76. *Id.*

77. Ericsson, *Deliberate* Practice, supra at 694.

78. COLVIN, *supra* note , at 67.

79. *Id.* at 69. ("Top performers repeat their practice activities to a stultifying extent.").

80. *Id.* at 70.

81. *Id.* ("Deliberate practice is above all an effort of focus and concentration.").

82. *Id.* at 71 ("After each repetition, we force ourselves to see–or get others to tell us–exactly what still isn't right so we can repeat the most painful and difficult parts of what we've just done. *Id.* at 71-72.).

83. MARZANO, *supra* at 7.

84. Colvin, *supra*.

85. *Id.*

86. Jennifer M. Cooper & Regan A. R. Gurung, *Smarter Law Study Habits: An Empirical Analysis of Learning Strategies and Relationship with Law GPA*, 62 ST. LOUIS U. L.J. 361, 373 (2018).

87. *Id.* I have discerned from my classes that one reason novice law students fail is because they lack this skill.

88. *Id.* at 124.

89. *Id.*

90. SHELL, *supra* at 14.

91. *Id.*

92. *Id.*

93. MARYBETH HERALD, YOUR BRAIN AND LAW SCHOOL: A CONTEXT AND PRACTICE BOOK 59 (2014).

94. SHELL, *supra* at 12.

95. *Id.*

96. SUSAN A. AMBROSE ET.AL., HOW LEARNING WORKS: 7 RESEARCH-BASED PRINCIPLES FOR SMART TEACHING 491 (2010).

97. *Id.* at 49.

98. Tonya Kowalski, *True North: Navigating for the Transfer of Learning in Legal Education*, 51 SEATTLE U. L. REV. 51, 51, 79 (2010).

99. Halpern, *supra* at 453.

100. *Id.* The brain organizes information in data structures in long-term memory ("schemata"). Schwartz, *Teaching Law Students*, *supra* at 373 ("These structures contain slots, theoretically organized like a card catalogue, for each of a countless number of specific situations.") Schemata store information, procedures, and subprocedures. *Id.* (Comparing schemata to computer programs.).

101. Halpern, *supra* at 453.

102. *Id.*

103. *Id.*; see also Kowalski, *supra* at 54.

104. Louis N. Schulze, *Using Science to Build Better Learners: One School's Successful Efforts to Rai se Its Bar Passage Rates in an Era of Decline*, 28 https://papers.ssrn.com/sol3/papers.cfm?abstract_id=2960192 at 4-5.

105. Kowalski, *supra* at 55.

106. *Id.* at 65.

107. Halpern, *supra* at 453.

108. *Id.*

109. Schwartz, *supra* at 419.

110. Halpern, *supra* at 450.

111. *See generally,* EDWARD DE BONO, LATERAL THINKING CREATIVITY: STEP BY STEP (1970).

112. PATRICIA L. SMITH & TILLMAN J. RAGAN, INSTRUCTIONAL DESIGN 132 (Wiley 2d ed. 1999). Kristen Holmquist describes the process in a slightly different way: "Cognitive psychologists define a problem, simply, as any situation in which the current state of affairs varies from the desired end point. And solving that problem entails a series of decisions and actions, each building on the last, in order to move the world closer to the goal state. In order to make these decisions, or encourage others to, we rely on stock stories, or schemas, familiar stories and arguments that act as heuristics and allow us to create meaning through narrative. . . . Lawyers as problem solvers rely on legal – and cultural – stocks in order to try to move the world in directions that benefit their clients. This movement involves persuasion of one form or

another – whether it's persuading a court to find for one's client, an opposing party in litigation to see one's settlement offer as a good deal, or collaborative party to undertake some kind of a joint venture." Kristen Holmquist, *Challenging Carnegie*, 61 J. L.EDUC. 353, 368-69 (2010). She adds, "On the most obvious level, legal precedent serves this function. . . . But lawyering involves appealing to stories and arguments that are relevant and persuasive for larger empirical, cultural, and social reasons, as well." *Id.* at 371. As I mentioned in Chapter Two, case briefs are schemas for understanding the law. When a lawyer problem solves, she draws on these schemas.

113. Michael Hunter Schwartz, *Teaching Law by Design: How Learning Theory and Instructional Design Can Inform and Reform Law Teaching*, 38 San. Diego L. Rev. 347, 397 (2001).

114. This model is based on a model at About.com: Psychology. Http://psychology.about.com/od/problemsolving/f/problem-solving-steps.htm.

115. The right attitude. If you adopt the attitude that "I will become a self-regulated learner" everything else will fall into place. Of course, this will take time. Rome was not built in a day. If you said self-control, you were close, but attitude is the beginning for all learning. If you have the right attitude, you can develop self-control.

Chapter Six
What to Expect in Law School

Chapter Goals.

1. To show you what to expect from and how to do well in doctrinal classes.
2. To introduce you to law school exams.
3. To discuss cooperative learning and study groups.
4. To tell you what to expect from legal writing classes.
5. To tell you what to expect from legal research class.
6. To talk about law school activities.
7. To discuss getting grades.
8. To talk about summer jobs.
9. To warn you about social media.
10. To introduce you to law school journals.
11. To stress the importance of the honor code.

I. Doing Well In Doctrinal Classes.

Many students hold a misconception concerning the law school class-room. Professor Leamnson has noted, "The most common misconception is that the class period is that occasion when the instructor tells you what you need to know to pass the tests."[1] This attitude does not lead to effective learning. As you should have learned in earlier chapters, this kind of attitude does not lead to effective learning because it is extrinsic motivation. Moreover, it gives the impression that law school is just about memorization. Law school is about learning the law, analyzing the law, synthesizing the law, and applying the synthesized law to a set of facts. In particular, if you do not apply the law to the facts well, you will do poorly on exams.

In addition, law school is cumulative. You will use skills you learned in one class in later classes. If you do not learn basic legal reasoning skills in your first semester of law school, you will struggle throughout the rest of law school and probably fail the bar. I have seen this happen many times.

Law schools generally include contracts, torts, property, criminal law, and civil procedure in the first year. Some law schools include constitutional law in the second semester or give you a choice of electives. Some first-year courses will be one semester, while others will be two. (This depends on the particular law school.) Your doctrinal classes will meet two or three times a week for two to four hours (total). Most law schools limit absences–generally no more than one absence per semester hour. (This rule should be irrelevant. You should try to attend every class so you don't fall behind.)

Law school classes require a lot of preparation. Professors will assign between twenty and fifty pages per class. (Ugh!) Your professors will expect you to be able to discuss the cases in class in detail. Moreover, if you do not know the cases well, you will get little out of the class.

Law school classes generally consist of lecture and Socratic questioning. The Socratic method is questioning a student in order to draw the answer out of him or her. Many law students consider the Socratic method a type of Medieval torture. Try not to adopt this attitude. Welcome your professor's questions; they will help you develop your legal reasoning skills. Some professors cold-call, while others ask for volunteers. Volunteer as much as possible. Again, this helps you develop your legal reasoning skills.

The questions could be on any facet of a case–the facts, issue, procedure, holding, or reasoning. The best and hardest questions are on a case's reasoning. Your professor will ask you how the judge got from the issue to the holding by applying the law to the facts. Your professor may also ask you to synthesize a rule from several cases. He or she may also ask you hypotheticals based on the main case. For example, "would the outcome of the case have differed if the offeree had been intoxicated at the time the contract was signed."

As I have written previously, give your full attention to class. Multi-tasking is a myth.[2] Also as mentioned earlier, be an active learner and listener in class. Mentally prepare yourself to listen in class. Determine what is important. Take notes selectively; don't write down everything. Relate material to prior knowledge. (How is battery in criminal law like battery in torts? How is it different?) Question in your head everything your professor or classmates say. Think of the implications of what is being said. Think up hypotheticals. Participate in the discussion!

Some professors will do things differently than the traditional methods laid out above. Some professors will do exercises in class–problem-solving. Others will go even further and use a "flipped" classroom. A flipped classroom is where your professor will ask you to read and learn materials before class and/or ask you to watch videos. Then, you will use this knowledge to do problem-solving in class. Flipped classrooms are active classrooms, which leads to much greater learning.

Law students often worry about giving the wrong answer in class. No one wants to embarrass themselves. As I have said before, making mistakes is part of learning. More importantly, the other students aren't paying much

114

attention to you; they are worried about making mistakes themselves. (Believe me; I went to law school.)

Finally, if you are confused, don't hesitate to ask questions. If you are still confused at the end of class, go up to talk to your professor or go to an office hour.

II. Law School Exams

While worrying too much about exams can hurt your learning, law school exams are still important. Everyone wants to do well in law school. I don't blame you for this; it is only natural.

In many classes, there will only be one exam, and, I admit that this can be scary. Some first-year professors give mid-terms, mainly to give you an introduction to what law school exams are like. (Thank them for this.)

Before you start taking exams, develop a method of time management. Doing well on one question, but failing to complete the last question will not get you a good grade. One method is, before you start writing your answers, think how long you can spend on a particular question. If all questions are of equal value, this will be easy. If you have three questions on a three-hour exam, devote an hour to each question. Some professors give different points to different questions. If one question is 50 points and the other two are 25 each on a three hour exam, devote 90 minutes to the 50 point question and 45 minutes each to the other two.

Most law school exams consist of essays and/or multiple choice questions. A typical essay question requires you to apply the law to the facts. Occasionally, you will be given the law, but most of the time you will have memorized it. Read the question carefully, so that you understand what your professor is looking for. Many students get low grades on exams because they start writing their answer before they understand the question. Don't include material not requested by the question. Some students try to write everything they know even if it is not relevant. This will lose you, rather than gain you, points.

An important aspect of successfully answering a law school essay question is issue spotting (identifying the legal/factual problem). Some questions have one issue; others many. Answer all material issues. Make sure you include your reasoning in your answer. ("Because" is the most important word in a law school exam question.) A law school exam answer is like a math answer in high school or college. Your professor is more interested in how you got to the solution, than the actual solution.

How to Succeed in Law School

Make sure you identify all material facts, and their legal significance within the question. You should underline the key facts in the question so you won't forget them. Make sure you apply the law to the facts in detail, rather than just giving a bare conclusion.

<u>Make sure you organize your answers well</u>. A typical model is Law-Reasoning/Application-Conclusion. You don't need to restate the facts in detail; your professor knows them; he wrote the question.

Multiple choice questions are not just a test of your memory. Good law school multiple choice questions test your legal reasoning ability and ability to apply the law to the facts. (Are you seeing a pattern yet?) Multiple choice questions are not easy; you must thoroughly know and understand the content of the course. Read each question and each answer carefully. Look for the issue and the material facts. Try to answer the question before you look at the answers. Then, read all answers. Don't stop with the first answer if it seems to be the right one. Answers often differ in the details. If you are struggling on a question, eliminate those answers that are clearly wrong and concentrate on the answers that might be right. If you are having difficulty with a question, skip and come back to it. Remember time management is important.

Example

Problem. Peggy complained several times about a broken lock on her apartment building's front door. Despite the fact that he knew the building was in a dangerous neighborhood, the landlord failed to fix the lock. Sven, a resident of the building, propped the front door of the apartment door open as he was moving out. While the door was propped open, a thief entered the building and stole Peggy's television and computer. Can Peggy recover from her landlord for negligence?

A. No. A landlord does not owe a duty to his tenants to protect their property.

B. No. Sven's negligence was a superceding cause.

C. No. Peggy should have bought a better lock for her door.

D. Yes. In most jurisdictions, a landlord is strictly liable for the safety of his tenants.

Answer. B.

Answering this question not only requires you to know the rules on landlord liability, it requires you to now how to apply the law to the facts.

Some professors allow open book exams. Don't be fooled. <u>Open book exams are just as hard as closed book ones</u>. You need to study as hard.

III. Cooperative Learning

Cooperative learning has become a buzz word in legal education. <u>Many professors like to have students do exercises together because they think it aids learning and because it helps them learn how to work together when they become lawyers</u>. And, for the most part, it does work, as long as it's not overdone and the professor supervises it closely to make sure that there are no freeloaders. Always participate fully in cooperative learning.

What I mainly want to talk about, though, is <u>cooperation in studying</u>. It has been traditional in law schools that students form study groups. This goes back to the dark ages when I was in law school. In addition to the below, study groups can help you improve your confidence; in study groups, you discover that other students are having the same problems as you are.

<u>The problem with most study groups is that students don't use them effectively, and they become a waste of time</u>. Study groups generally help their members prepare for class and review for exams. Often, they end up doing what each student should be doing on their own. For example, study groups often divide up the chore of outlining a class. However, having an outline of a class is not what's important; it is doing the outline yourself. Doing a class outline helps you remember things better, and it helps develop your skills, such as case synthesis. (How does this fit with the neurobiology of learning?)

<u>There is much that study groups can do for you</u>. Study groups can be like a class where students discuss the cases. (This isn't enough time to develop your discussion skills in a large first-year class.) Students can improve their critical skills. After your group discusses a case, a member can come up with a dissent, and the others can critique it. Study groups or even just two students can criticize cases, do problem-solving exercises, and give each other hypotheticals. In other words, <u>study groups can help students become self-regulated learners</u>. Students can also interact using Twitter, boards, blogs, or text messaging.

<u>I believe that the best study groups involve just two students</u>. This allows each person to become more involved. A good technique for one-on-one meetings is think aloud exercises, a way of doing hypotheticals. In a typical think-aloud session, the student "talks through" a problem with his teacher or another student.[3] During the think aloud, the student verbalizes all

117

steps of the thinking process, including alternatives and dead ends. Think-aloud exercises help students develop problem-solving skills, reflect on their problem-solving strategies, deal with new types of problems, and improve domain-transfer skills.[4] You can think up hypotheticals for think alouds or use old exam questions from the law library. In other words, think-alouds will significantly improve your exam taking ability.

IV. Legal Writing

Legal writing may be the most important course you take in law school. This is because lawyers write more than they do anything else. Attorneys write memos, briefs, letters to clients, contracts, wills, and many other documents. In litigation, cases are often won or lost on the pleadings. I know that you have a concept of exciting trials from television and the movies, but most cases never reach the trial stage.

Early in your career you will be judged on how well you write. Your potential employers will ask to see a writing sample. Summer associates and young lawyers write, while more experienced lawyers go to court, meet with clients, and negotiate deals. Do you think you are going to argue a death penalty case your first week as a lawyer?

Legal writing at most law schools is two semesters for two or three credits. A few law schools have additional semesters of required legal writing, sometimes combined with other skills, such as client counseling or negotiation.

A key part of legal writing is learning how to analyze legal materials. You will be taught how to find issues, "brief" (analyze) a case, and synthesize cases into a legal rule. You will also be taught how to apply the law to the facts. At some point, your professor will introduce statutory analysis.

The typical first-semester writing course focuses on objective writing. A typical example is an objective memorandum in which you objectively evaluate a problem. In other words, you are given a set of facts, and you are expected to (objectively) come to a conclusion based on those facts. The first major assignment will generally be a "closed" memo. With a closed memo, you are given the materials you need for the analysis. Most professors have you write a first draft, they will meet with you concerning the first draft, then you will rewrite it. Revision is an important part of legal writing. It helps you improve from your mistakes.

Next, you will write an open memo for which you will have to do the research. Otherwise, the process is the same as with the closed memo.

The second semester of legal writing focuses on <u>persuasive writing</u>. With persuasive writing you are trying to convince someone–usually the court–that your argument is the correct one. The major differences between what you learn in the second semester and the first one is that your writing should be persuasive, rather than objective, and that you must follow the court's formatting rules.

The major assignment for this semester is an <u>appellate brief</u>. Typically, you will write a brief as if you are writing it for the Supreme Court. This may sound daunting, but your professor will explain the process step-by-step.

The other major part of the second semester is <u>moot court</u>–arguing your brief as if you were arguing it before the Supreme Court. Most students look forward to moot court because they get to dress up and act like real lawyers. Again, your professors will fully explain how to argue before an appellate court.

To end, let me add one important piece of advice about legal writing: Don't get behind!! Start your research early; don't wait to the last minute to write the brief. Give yourself time to reflect on the problem.

V. Legal Research Class

<u>In legal research class, you will be taught to find the sources (materials) of the law</u>. <u>Law is based on authority</u>. You have to back up your arguments with cases, statutes, and other material. Therefore, the ability to find the right statute or the best case is vital to effective lawyering.

Legal research is sometimes taught in legal writing class. At some law schools, it is taught by law librarians in a separate class. It generally meets once or twice a week.

When I went to law school in the last millennium, legal research was mainly done in books–digests, reporters, statute books, etc. Each year since then, computer-based/online research has become more important. However, I believe that it is important to learn both online and book research methods. It is easy to make mistakes with online research, and the methods of book research help you develop your legal reasoning skills.

Here are the most important things to understand about legal research:

1. Don't stop until you have found all the relevant materials. The last case you find may be the best one.

2. Good research wins cases. Lazy researchers lose cases.

3. Always double-check your research, such as cite checking.

4. Always double-check your research the day you file your brief. New materials come out everyday.

VI. Law School Activities

All law schools offer many educational and social activities. You will want to participate in some of these activities, but don't over-extend yourself.

Educational activities help you develop skills you may not have learned in class. Moot court and trial competitions for second- and third-year students are both fun and educational. Participating in them shows employers that you have the skills they want.

Law school career and academic support offices offer many classes on how to succeed in law school, how to get a job, and wellness. It is smart to take advantage of these classes, but again don't over extend yourself.

Law school student bar associations and specialized groups offer frequent social activities. Your purpose in coming to law school hopefully is not to socialize, but you do need to relax and have fun sometimes. However, avoid drugs and excessive drinking.

Let me repeat again that if you need help go to one of the professionals at your law school. They are there to help. There is no stigma in seeking help; the real problem is to let the problem grower larger. (I will discuss wellness in depth in Chapter Eight.)

VII. Getting Your Grades

Waiting for law school grades is torture. When I was in law school, we all lined up in front of student records at 11 a.m. the Friday before the beginning of the second-semester classes. Student records handed each of us our first-semester grades. I ran off to a isolated corner to open my grades. I opened my grades, and . . . Okay, you don't really want to know what my first-semester grades were, but I want you to know that all of us have experienced the stress of waiting.

Today, it is better and worse. Grades are generally posted online. At most law schools, grades trickle out. Torts grades might be posted two weeks before Contracts grades. To me, this seems worse than getting them all at one time. If you receive a low Torts grade, you will worry more about the rest of your grades.

DON'T pester your professor about your grades. This will only make things worse.

If you receive a low grade in a class, talk to the professor about what you did wrong on the exam. This will help you learn what to do on the next set of exams. Don't act angry at your professor about your grade. 99% of the time, a low grade is the students' fault. If your professor has made a mathematical error or other obvious error, do politely point that out. I once had a friend who received a letter that he had failed the Kentucky bar exam. He went to a bar examiner to go over his test. While going over his test the examiner noticed that the individual scores had been added up incorrectly. People do make mistakes.

All law schools today have academic support offices. The personnel in these offices are there to help struggling students. If you did poorly on several exams, go to your academic support office so that they can help you with exam-taking techniques.

VIII. Summer Jobs

Summer jobs provide experience and usually pay. Whether you can get a summer job after your first year of law school depends on the economy. After my first year, the economy was good, and most of us obtained summer jobs. A couple of years later, the economy went into a recession, and summer jobs were hard to find.

Summer legal jobs run the gamut of possibilities. One summer I worked for a small commercial law firm; the next summer I worked in the legal department of KFC. I had friends who worked for large law firms, for the government, and for charitable organizations. The possibilities are endless (as long as the economy is good.) I advise that you to try to get different jobs each summer so you have a better idea of what being a lawyer is.

The ideal job for many is to work for a large law firm. The pay is very good, and it often leads to a permanent job at that firm. However, if you don't like that type of work, do what you want to do; it is your life.

Some summer jobs are low paying or don't pay at all (unpaid internships). This presents a dilemma; do you want to accept such a job? If it is an organization you support, such as a charity, this may only be a minor problem. However, what if it is just a typical summer legal job–neither very good or very bad. Experience is experience, and employers look for experience when you go for your first full-time job. However, this can be a real problem when you need to earn money for law school. You may have to take the well-paying non-legal job over the legal job.

How do you get a summer job? Let me count the ways. The usual advice is networking. Do you or a family member have a friend who is a lawyer who could use extra help in the summer? Of course, your law school career services office has many resources on obtaining summer jobs. Not only do they list job opportunities, they can give you advice on how to obtain a job in your area. Although this might seem premature, you probably should talk with someone in career services about summer jobs early in your first semester. Of course, they will probably have workshops for first years about summer jobs.

I have one piece of advice about interviewing for summer jobs. <u>Always act professionally.</u> <u>The reputation you make now will follow you throughout your legal career.</u>

IX. Social Media

Be <u>very</u> caseful how you use social media! Much of what is on social media stays on the internet forever. It seems like every week, a politician or celebrity is getting into trouble for what they said on social media; sometimes for what they said many years ago.

As I was revising this section I ran across this:

A survivor of the Marjory Stoneman Douglas High School shooting said Monday that Harvard University has rescinded his acceptance after recently surfaced screenshots showed him using racial slurs a few months before the 2018 massacre in Parkland, Fla. Kyle Kashuv, 18, who was admitted to Harvard earlier this year, wrote on Twitter that he had been made aware of "egregious and callous comments" he made when he was 16 years old. A survivor of the Marjory Stoneman Douglas High School shooting said Monday that Harvard University has rescinded his acceptance after recently surfaced screenshots showed him using racial slurs a few months before the 2018 massacre in Parkland, Fla. Kyle Kashuv, 18, who was admitted to Harvard earlier this year, wrote on Twitter that he had been made aware of "egregious and callous comments" he made when he was 16 years old. Classmates had accused him of repeatedly using the N-word, according to The Washington Times and

HuffPost.[5]

Before you post anything on social media, stop to think what effect it might have in the future. Something that is funny today may damage your career many years from now. The best attitude to adopt now is that "I am a professional," and "I will act like one." (Of course, this applies to all your activities. For example, you can drink in public, but you should not be drunk in public. Similarly, anything you say in public can be overhead. Some celebrities have even gotten into trouble for what they said in private to their spouses or friends.)

Right now, review your social media history, and erase anything you can that might be considered offensive.

X. Journals

Many of you will want to be on a journal. Law schools usually have a main journal and several secondary ones. The main journal is generally a general journal, while the secondary journals are specialized journals, such as journals on intellectual property or education law.

A school's main journal is the most prestigious one; big law employers usually hire editors and members of the main journal. However, experience on the secondary journals can also be valuable, especially with mid-level employers. All employers favor applicants with writing experience.

How one obtains membership on a journal varies by law school, so check your law school's website for the exact process. At most law schools, the law school competition process occurs right after second-semester finals. Usually applicants are judged on two grounds: 1) first-year grades and 2) a write-on competition. The write-on competition requires you to do analytical writing, such as a case note. (A case note is an analysis of a case.)

Don't be disappointed if you didn't get selected for the main journal or a secondary one. As I mentioned above, there are many other activities to do in law school, such as moot court teams and trial practice teams that can provide you with practical experience.

XI. The Honor Code

Law schools take their honor codes very seriously. <u>Law schools do not tolerate cheating, plagiarism, and other misconduct</u>. I know of several students whose legal careers were ended or damaged by honor code violations.

For example, I once heard a story of a student who was expelled from his law school because the police arrested him with a gun on the front seat of his car.

Read your school's honor code the first week of law school or earlier. Make sure you understand it thoroughly. Make sure you understand what plagiarism means. (Using someone else's work without attribution.) Also, make sure you know what other conduct is forbidden. Bullying will get you into as much trouble as cheating.

Law school professors may add their own requirements in addition to the honor code. At one law school, the professor had a requirement that students must write at the end of their exams: "I did not cheat on this exam, and I did not miss more than three classes." A student mentioned to the professor that three students had missed more than three classes. Those students were required to drop the class before the exam. Similarly, a student went to a law school administrator to say that two students had misrepresented their attendance on the class attendance book. All actions have consequences.

Cheating is most common in legal writing. Because students work outside of class, they think they can get by with cheating, such as by working together on papers or plagiarizing. These students are wrong. I caught several students cheating during my fifteen years of teaching legal writing. These students failed the class, had to take it again, and they had a notation on their records. Most importantly, they had to tell prospective employers why they failed legal writing if they were asked. Finally, many legal writing professors use anti-plagiarism software. Don't endanger your future career by doing something stupid.

Notes

1. Robert Leamnson, *Learning (You First Job)*, https://www1.udel.edu/CIS/106/iaydin/07F/misc/firstJob.pdf. at 3.

2. Shailini Jandial George, Teaching the Smartphone Generation: How Cognitive Science Can Improve Learning in Law School, 66 Maine L.Rev. 163, 177-79 (2017).

3. MICHAEL HUNTER SCHWARTZ & DENISE RIEBE, CONTRACTS: A CONTEXT AND PRACTICE CASEBOOK 719-20 (2009); *see also* Stefan H. Krieger & Serge Martinez, *Performance Isn't Everything: The Importance of Conceptual Competence in Outcome Assessment of Experiential Learning*, 19 CLINICAL L. REV. 251 (2012); BRIAN P. COPPOLA, *Progress in Practice: Using Concepts from Motivational and Self-Regulated Learning Research to Improve Chemistry Instruction*, in NEW DIRECTIONS FOR TEACHING AND LEARNING: UNDERSTANDING SELF-REGULATED LEARNING NO. 63, 89-90 (1995). Professors Schwartz and Riebe include several think-aloud exercises in their contracts book.

4. Professors McNamara and Magliano have asserted, "[t]he reading strategies that readers engage in while self-explaining or thinking aloud are heavily guided by metacognition." Danielle S. McNamara & Joseph P. Magliano, *Self-Explanation and Metacognition, in* HANDBOOK OF METACOGNITION 61 (2009).

5. https://thehill.com/homenews/news/448866-harvard-rescinds-acceptance-to-parkland-survivor-kyle-kashuv-over-past-comments.

Chapter Seven
Context for Law School

Chapter Goals.

1. To give you context for your legal studies.
2. To tell you how our legal system developed.
3. To introduce you to the three sources of American law.
4. To give you examples of the five types of legal reasoning.
5. To show the role of ambiguity in our legal system.
6. To introduce you to the structure of the American court system.
7. To introduce mandatory (binding) and persuasive authority.
8. To introduce the steps in a civil case.

When I started law school, I felt like I had been thrown into the middle of a lake. I had no context for what we were doing. On orientation, we had a one-hour session on case briefing, but that was it. I didn't know why on the first day we discussing cases about intentional torts or reading about who gets ownership over a wild animal. Sink or swim, and a lot of my classmates sank.

It is better today, but you still don't get a lot of context before you start to read and discuss cases.

I. The Three Sources of Law

Let me begin with a story. It is a simplified story on how the Anglo-American legal system developed. It will help you understand what is going on in your classes.

In the Middle Ages, the English kings expanded their territory. They needed to develop a system to help them govern that territory. In other words, they needed to create a system of law. Now, they had two choices. Many countries had civil law systems. In a civil law system, the legal system is centered around written rules–a code, which governs conduct. This system had judges, but they were bound by the written rules. A civil system gives the governed a great deal of security concerning the rules they must follow, but it doesn't allow for much flexibility. In other words, civil law systems are written in stone, like the Code of Hammurabi.

The English kings tried something different. Instead of a rigid statutory code, they allowed judges to create the law on case-by-case basis. This is called the common law, judge-made law, or case law. Under the common law, disputants take their claims to a judge, and the judge decides the case. His decision then becomes precedent for future similar cases.

For example, a man is fascinated with wild animals, and he wants to keep a tiger on his property. There are no rules that prevent him from owning a tiger. He builds a strong cage so the tiger can't escape. Nevertheless, the tiger escapes and kills his neighbor's cow. The neighbor (the plaintiff) sues the tiger owner (the defendant). [Case 1] The neighbor argues: "Defendant brought a wild tiger onto his property, and it escaped and killed my cow. He should have to pay me $1,000 for the cost of my cow." "Oh no," shouts the defendant, "I was very careful to make sure that my tiger could not escape. I built the strongest possible cage. Therefore, I was not negligent, and courts, in the Anglo-American legal system only give damages for intentional torts and negligence." "But, your honor," replies the plaintiff, "My cow is dead, I have suffered a loss, and it was the defendant who brought a wild animal into our neighborhood."

The judge considers both sides' arguments and rules for the plaintiff, awarding him $1,000." The judge declares, "There is no precedent for this case. It is a case of first impression. Therefore, I will have to decide this case based on policy. Both parties are innocent; neither did anything wrong. However, the defendant did bring a wild animal on to his property, and I believe that he should be liable for the loss. I shall call the basis of this ruling 'strict liability." The holding from Case 1 would be "when a person brings a wild animal onto his property, and it escapes causing property damage, the animal owner will be strictly liable (liable without fault) for those damages."

The tiger owner makes the tiger's cage even stronger. However, the tiger escapes and bites his neighbor, causing him $1,000 in hospital bills. His neighbor sues the tiger owner. [Case 2] The neighbor argues, "His tiger escaped, and bit my arm, causing me $1,000 in hospital costs. Based on the strict liability rules from Case 1, this court should rule for me and award me $1,000 for my losses. Here, the plaintiff is arguing from precedent. The facts of Case 2 are like the facts of Case 1, so this court should apply the rule from Case 1 to Case 2. "Hold on, hold on," yells the defendant. Case 1 and Case 2 are distinguishable. [The facts of Case 2 are different from the facts of Case 1, so the court should not apply the rule from Case 1 to Case 2.] Case 1 involved property damage, while Case 2 involves personal injury." The judge states, "I have heard the arguments of both parties. I think that Case 2 is similar to Case 1 so I find for the defendant and awarded him $1,000. The key point is that a wild animal escaped and caused damages in both cases.

The differences between property damages and personal injury are not material." From Case 1 and Case 2, we can synthesize a rule "when a person brings a wild animal onto his property, and it escapes causing personal injury or property damage, the animal owner will be strictly liable (liable without fault) for those damages." (To synthesize the rule, I looked at the similarities and differences between the cases' facts and outcomes and determined how they affected the outcome.)

A woman loves pit bulls. However, pit bills can be aggressive, so she does everything she can to make sure her pit bull does not escape. However, the pit bull does escape, and bites the neighbor, costing him $1,000 in hospital bills. The neighbor sues the pit bull owner. [Case 3] The neighbor states, "My neighbor owns a pit bull that escaped and bit me, causing $1,000 in hospital bills. This case is governed by the precedent of the tiger cases so the strict liability rule should be applied to my case. [reasoning by analogy; precedent]. The pit bull owner asserts, "Your honor, this case is not like the tiger cases. A tiger is a wild animal, a pit bull is a pet. You should not apply the strict liability rule to this case. [distinguishing cases] Since I was not negligent, you should find for me." The judge rules: "I find for the plaintiff, and award her $1,000. It is true that pit bulls are not wild animals. However, like tigers, pit bulls can be dangerous." [Notice how the judge found the cases similar based on the details. Details are important in the law.] New synthesis: "When a person brings a dangerous animal onto his property, and it escapes causing personal injury or property damage, the animal owner will be strictly liable (liable without fault) for those damages." [Notice the subtle change in the synthesized holding caused by Case 3. This is how the common law develops.]

Grandma owns a toy poodle, Fluffy. Fluffy is a gentle animal. However, one day when friends are visiting, a child explodes a fire cracker near Fluffy, she becomes frightened, and she bites the plaintiff. The plaintiff sues grandma. [Case 4] The plaintiff argues: "Fluffy bit me, causing $1,000 in hospital bills. Under the synthesized rule from Cases 1,2, and 3, this court should hold grandma liable for my damages under strict liability." Grandma disagrees: "This case is not like tiger cases or the pit bull case. Fluffy is a gentle animal. The other cases involved known-dangerous animals. Therefore, those cases are distinguishable from the present one." The judge rules for grandma: "Toy poodles are not like the known-dangerous animals involved in Cases 1-3. The policy behind those rules is that a person who brings a known-dangerous animal onto her property is strictly liable for damages caused by those animals because they brought the danger to the neighborhood.

Toy poodles are known as gentle, friendly animals. I find for the defendant."
[The judge distinguished the prior cases based on both facts and policy.] New
synthesis: "When a person brings a known-dangerous animal onto his
property, and it escapes causing personal injury or property damage, the animal owner will be strictly liable (liable without fault) for those damages."
[Again, Case 4 caused a subtle change in the synthesized rule.]

The above example illustrates how common law develops. Notice the
different types of legal reasoning used by the judges: policy-based reasoning,
applying precedent (reasoning by analogy), distinguishing cases and rules (the
opposite of reasoning by analogy), and synthesizing rules.[1]

Case-based reasoning continued for several hundred years. Eventually, the nobles gained greater power, and they wanted to curtail the king's
power. They did this by establishing a legislature (Parliament). A legislature
enacts statutes (written laws). (What type of reasoning do statutes usually
involve?) Because they are intended to limit the king's power, judges must
follow statutes. In other words, if the legislative rule is different than a judge-
made rule (case law), the judge must follow the statute. However, a judge
applies statutes (by rule-based reasoning), interprets statutes (determines the
meaning of the statute), and, when constitutions were enacted, the judge could
rule that a particular statute was unconstitutional. (Case law remains valid in
the absence of a statute.)

This system continued for several hundred years, with most cases
being governed by case law, but with a few governed by statute. As time went
on, statutes became more important. Eventually, society became more complex, and administrative law (law made by the executive branch) came into
existence. Administrative law was needed because a legislature didn't have
time to deal with everything, and legislators are not experts in all areas. Today, there are administrative agencies on federal and state levels. The Federal
Communications Commission makes rules for television and radio. The Food
and Drug Administration makes sure our food is safe. The Ministry of Silly
Walks makes rules about silly walks. (This was a Monty Python skit. If you
haven't seen it, look for it on You Tube. It is hilarious. I give this as an
example because there are agencies that cover many, many subjects, even very
narrow ones.)

On the federal level, Congress delegates authority to administrative
agencies to make rules (regulations) in their areas of expertise under the
Administrative Procedure Act. (You do not have to worry about the rule
making process in your first year.) Judges interpret administrative rules, make

sure that the agency has the power to promulgate the rule, determine that the agency promulgated the rule with the proper process, and establish the constitutionality of the rules.

In sum, there are three sources of law in the Anglo-American legal system:

1. Judge-made rules.
2. Statutes enacted by the legislature.
3. Administrative regulations.

Of course, in our system, all of these are governed by the Constitution.

All three of these sources are important for our modern system. However, statutes and administrative regulations have replaced judge-made law in many areas. Your classes will start with judge-made law because, as you can see from the above story, judge-made law is the foundation of our legal system. You will have some introduction to statutory interpretation during your first year. Most law schools do not bring in administrative law until the second and third years.

Exercises

1. What are the three sources of law in the American legal system?
2. How did the American legal system develop?
3. What is reasoning by precedent?
4. What is reasoning by analogy?
5. What is distinguishing cases?
6. What is rule-based reasoning?
7. How do you synthesize rules?
8. What is policy-based reasoning?
9. Do judges have to follow statutes?
10. What is a judge's role in connection with statutes?
11. What is a judge's role in connection with administrative regulations?
12. Read the Wikipedia entry on a federal administrative agency, such as the Federal Trade Commission.

II. Don't be Afraid of Ambiguity

The law is ambiguous. American law is not a set of rigid rules that are completely clear. Rather, American law involves interpretation and reinterpretation. It is constantly changing. Old rules get rejected, and other rules are reinterpreted because of different facts and changing policies.

The Anglo-American legal system was intended to evolve based on changing circumstances. Parties bring a case to a court, and that case becomes precedent for future cases. A new case on different facts uses that rule, but it changes it some because of the new facts. This process continues on and on. Statutes are written rules, but they too are subject to interpretation, and the legislature is constantly passing new statutes and repelling old ones..

In addition, language is not exact. Most words have multiple definitions, and the meaning of words are affected by their context. Moreover, not all judges are great writers. Finally, the ambiguity in the law helps it develop. Finally, a rule or statute cannot anticipate all possible occurrences.

Most new law students are bothered by the law's ambiguity. They want the law to be clear so that it is easier to memorize and apply. However, ambiguity is central to American law, and you should embrace it. Ambiguity allows lawyers to make legal arguments. Without ambiguity, the court could just type the facts into a computer; voila, the right decision. Lawyers would be unnecessary. You would have to go to medical school and get all kinds of icky stuff on your hands.

Lawyers use ambiguity to argue the facts in their clients' favor. Similarly, lawyers use ambiguity to show how the law favors their clients' legal position. (You will learn how to use ambiguity in legal writing.)

Exercises

1. Is the world black and white or shades of gray? Answer the same question concerning the law?

2. Do you have trouble dealing with ambiguity? Does it make you feel uncomfortable?

3. Think of courses you took in college: which ones involved ambiguity and which ones didn't?

3. Why is ambiguity important in the law?

4. Is there always one right answer in the law? Why do courts in different jurisdictions come to different conclusions based on similar facts?

(Yes, the laws of different jurisdictions often differ on the same facts. For example, some jurisdictions had comparative negligence while others had contributory negligence.)

5. Take a favorite story of yours and rewrite it from different points of view. For example, use Goldilocks and the Three Bears. Write it from Goldilocks point of view. Write it from the Papa Bear's point of view. The Momma Bear's. The Baby Bear's. How would a newspaper report the story?
6. Take a policy position you hold strongly, and write an opposing position.
7. How did ambiguity affect the four cases (wild animal cases) above?

III. The Structure of the American Court System

The United States has two concurrent court systems–the federal system is established by the United States Constitution and Congress, and the state systems are established by state constitutions. The federal system is a three-tiered system, comprising the federal districts courts, the courts of appeals, and the Supreme Court. Cases are generally brought in the district court. Each state has at least one district court; more populous states have more. (For example, New York is divided into four federal districts.) Federal courts are courts of limited jurisdiction. This means that only certain types of cases can be brought in federal court. (You will learn the rules of federal jurisdiction in your Civil Procedure class). Also, certain cases must be brought in the federal courts, such as copyright cases. ("exclusive juris-diction") You also have to file in the proper venue (location). (You will also learn venue rules in Civil Procedure.)

When the case is final (it has been terminated by trial or some other procedure), the losing party has one right of appeal (assuming that party has reasonable grounds for appeal). An appeal must be filed with the proper appellate court. For example, you would appeal a case from the Southern District of New York to the United States Court of Appeals for the Second Circuit. Courts of appeals exist to correct errors of lower courts. You do not retry your case in an appellate court. You need to present an issue or issues based on errors of the lower court to the appellate court. The appellate court will issue a decision based on the parties' briefs and oral arguments. If a party is dissatisfied with the intermediate appellate court's decision, that party can try to appeal to the Supreme Court by filing a writ of certiorari. The Supreme Court's jurisdiction is discretionary, which means that the court decides the cases it hears. The Supreme Court takes only a small percentage of cases (about 100 a year) that parties try to appeal to it. In other words, your need to make your best effort in front of the immediate court of appeals because this is probably your last chance. Like the intermediate appellate court, the Supreme Court decides the case based on the parties briefs and oral argument.

State court systems are similar to the federal system. Each state has its own court system. Some states have two-tired systems (one appellate court), but most have two. Each state names its courts differently, so don't get confused. For example, the trial court in New York is called the Supreme Court. (Very confusing.) State courts generally hear all types of cases, even ones based on federal statutes. As I mentioned above, jurisdiction is exclusive in the federal courts under a few statutes.

One more wrinkle in state courts. Most state courts have two kinds of trial courts. One set hears misdemeanors and cases under a certain amount (say $5,000), the other felonies and cases over a certain amount. The names of these courts differ greatly among the states so don't get confused when doing your reading.

The above are the basics of the American court system. You will learn much more detail in your Civil Procedure class.

Exercises

1. Why does the United States have two court systems?
2. What is the difference between a trial court and an appellate court?
3. What is the main function of an appellate court?
4. What do appellate courts base their decisions on?
5. How is this different from trial courts?
6. Can federal courts hear all cases?
7. Describe the structure of the federal system?
8. What is the likelihood that you will try a case in front of the Supreme Court?
9. How are state courts similar to federal courts? How are they different?
10. Can all cases be tried in state courts?
11. What are the two types of trial courts in state systems?

IV. Mandatory Versus Persuasive Authority

Legal argument is based on authority. You first present the law, explain the law, then you apply the law to the facts. Within this framework, you need to use the best law–the relevant statutes and the best cases. The relevant statutes are the statutes that govern in the jurisdiction whose law governs your case. The best cases have two characteristics: 1) you should start with mandatory authority, cases which the court must follow, and 2) you need to find the cases most on point (those cases which are most similar to your case).

This section will focus on mandatory and persuasive authority.

Mandatory (binding) cases are cases on point that come from the governing jurisdiction. For example, your case involves whether a contract has been accepted by the defendant. The state whose law governs is Indiana. Therefore, cases from Indiana that are current (they haven't been overruled) and on point are mandatory in your case.

Persuasive authority is everything else. Persuasive authority may be cases from other jurisdictions. Say in the above example, you have found a case that supports your position that has convincing reasoning from Oregon. Can you cite it to the court? Yes, unless there is mandatory authority from your jurisdiction that contradicts the persuasive case. Even then you can cite it if your are trying to get your court to overrule a precedent (make new judge-made law). Let's say the Oregon case is on point and that mandatory authority doesn't contradict it. How will it be treated by your court? The court may follow it, but it doesn't have to. In other words, if you want your court to follow it, you need to convince your court that the case's reasoning is strong.

Secondary sources are also persuasive authority. Secondary sources are commentary on the law, such as treatises, legal encyclopedias, and law review articles. Sources like treatises and encyclopedias generally give the general law–what the usual rule is in the United States. Thus, such sources can be very convincing to a court that lacks cases on a particular subject that has not been covered by that state's law. Because they are persuasive authority, courts can adopt the law from the secondary source, but it doesn't have to.

Reflect for a second on the difference between mandatory and persuasive authority.

The level of the court is also important for mandatory authority. Lower courts must follow the on point rulings of higher courts. That means that all federal courts must follow the rulings of the United States Supreme Court. Federal district courts must also follow the on point rulings of their appellate court. For example, courts in the Southern District of New York must follow the on point decisions of the Second Circuit. However, they don't have to follow the on point decisions of the Sixth Circuit. They can if they want to, but they don't have to. (Sixth Circuit decisions are persuasive authority for Second Circuit district courts.) In federal courts, courts do not have to follow the on point decisions of courts on the same level. For instance, The Sixth Circuit is not bound by decisions of the Second Circuit.

The effect of authority is similar with state courts. Authority from other states would be persuasive authority in that state's courts.

Now let me really confuse you. What is the effect of federal cases in state courts, and what is the effect of state cases in federal courts? Look for the jurisdiction whose law governs, and that jurisdiction's authority is mandatory. Say you have a case in Kentucky state court on whether a contract is valid. You find a great case on issue from the Western District of Kentucky, is that case mandatory or persuasive authority? Kentucky state law governs because the question of the validity of a contract is usually governed by state law. Therefore, the federal case is persuasive authority. The Kentucky court can adopt it, but it doesn't have to.

Say the contract case is in federal court. There is a case on point from the Kentucky Supreme Court, which hurts your case. Does the federal court have to follow it? Yes, because Kentucky courts are the lawmaker for cases that concern areas where Kentucky law governs. (I hope you can se that you need to develop the ability to determine which jurisdiction's law governs.)

The best way to get the above into your head is by doing exercises.

Exercises

1. A federal statute is the governing law in a case filed in state court. Does the state have to follow the federal statute?

2. Kentucky has a long-standing case rule on an issue of tort law. The legislature recently passed a statute that differs from the case law. Does the case or the statute control?

3. Congress enacted a statute in 2012. The U. S. Supreme Court recently concluded that the statute is unconstitutional. Does a state court in Kentucky have to follow the statute on a matter of federal law?

4. What do judges do in connection with statutes?

5. What if a judge disagrees with the wisdom of a statute?

6. There is a case in Kentucky court that involves an automobile accident connected completely with Kentucky. Tennessee recently passed an innovative statute that relates to the issue in dispute. What is the effect of the Tennessee statute?

Are the following cases mandatory or persuasive. Assume all cases are on point.

136

7. A Kentucky Supreme court case interpreting a situation covered by Kentucky common law in the U.S. District Court for the Western District of Kentucky.

8. A Kentucky Supreme court case interpreting a Kentucky statute in an Alaska trial court in which the Kentucky statute is the controlling law.

9. A Kentucky Supreme court case interpreting a Kentucky statute in a case before the U.S. Supreme Court in which the Kentucky statute is the controlling law.

10. A U.S. Supreme Court case interpreting a Kentucky statute in a case before the Kentucky Supreme Court.

11. A Kentucky Supreme Court case on Kentucky common law in the trial court of Jefferson County, Ky.

12. A Second Circuit case in a case in the U. S. District Court for the Central District of California.

13. A case from the Kentucky Supreme Court in a dispute involving Kansas common law in a Kansas trial court.

Answers

1. Yes. The federal statute is the governing law.
2. The statute. Statutes control over case law.
3. No. The U. S. Supreme Court ruled the statute unconstitutional.
4. They can interpret them, and they can hold them unconstitutional.
5. Tough luck. Judges have to follow statutes as long as they are constitutional.
6. Nothing. Kentucky courts do not have to follow statutes of other states in cases that only concern Kentucky. If a litigant brought it up, the judge would probably say that is a matter for the Kentucky legislature to decide.
7. Mandatory. The Kentucky Supreme Court is the lawmaker in this case.
8. Mandatory. Same reasoning. How did the case get to Alaska? Stranger things do happen.
9. Mandatory. Same reasoning.
10. Persuasive. I know you think of the U.S. Supreme Court as the top court in the United States, but this is only true for federal law. Of course, the U. S. Supreme Court can hold a state statute unconstitutional, but in that case it is applying federal law.
11. Mandatory. Lower courts must follow higher courts.
12. Persuasive. The Second Circuit is not in the line of appeal for the Central District of California. In other words, the Second Circuit is not a higher court

in relation to the Central District of California.

13. Persuasive. The Kansas court can follow it if it is convinced by the case's reasoning, but it doesn't have to (as long as there is not a Kansas case on point).

Note: In writing an objective memorandum or a brief to the court, you do not state whether a case is mandatory or persuasive. The reader should know this if you used the proper citation.

IV. The Anatomy of a Civil Case.

As a final bit of context before you start reading cases in law school, I will present how a civil case proceeds in American courts. This is important because it is hard to read a case for your classes unless you understand the procedure involved.

A case begins with the filing of a summons and complaint. A summons is just a document letting the defendant know she was sued and a little on what she should do. The complaint sets forth in numbered paragraphs what the suit is about. In *Bell Atlantic v. Twombly* (2007), the Supreme Court held that a complaint must include facts (as distinct from legal labels and "conclusions") giving rise to a plausible (rather than merely conceivable) entitlement to relief. A complaint ends with a prayer for relief. Look for a sample complaint on the internet.

The defendant has a set time to respond to the complaint, with the time being set forth in the jurisdiction's rules. (The summons will also generally state how much time there is to respond.) Defendants generally file an answer to a complaint. The answer comprises numbered paragraphs that respond to the numbered paragraphs in plaintiff's complaint. The responses generally consist of admit, deny, or lack sufficient knowledge to admit or deny. Answers also can include affirmative defenses and may include a counterclaim. Look for a sample answer on the internet. Instead of filing an answer, a defendant may file a motion to dismiss for failure to state a claim, a motion to dismiss for lack of subject matter jurisdiction, a motion to dismiss for lack of personal jurisdiction, a motion to dismiss for improper venue, a motion to dismiss for insufficient process, a motion to dismiss for insufficient service of process insufficient, motion to dismiss for failure to join a party under Rule 19, or a motion on the pleadings. Your civil procedure class will cover these motions. If you read a case in another class before you reach them, look up that motion in a legal dictionary so you can fully understand the case you are reading.

Assuming the case has not been dismissed on one of the above motions or has not been settled, the next step in a civil litigation is generally discovery (getting information from the otherside). The American court system wants cases decided on the truth, so most American courts allow for broad discovery. Discovery includes written interrogatories (questions), requests for production of documents, requests for admissions, and depositions. Your civil procedure class will cover each of these.

In addition to the above motions, a case may be terminated before trial by a motion for summary judgment. Under federal rule 56, "A party may move for summary judgment, identifying each claim or defense—or the part of each claim or defense—on which summary judgment is sought. The court shall grant summary judgment if the movant shows that there is no genuine dispute as to any material fact and the movant is entitled to judgment as a matter of law. The court should state on the record the reasons for granting or denying the motion." The best way to understand a rule or a statute is to break it into parts. In other words, for summary judgments, the moving party must establish two things: 1) there is no genuine dispute to any material fact and 2) the movant is entitled to judgment as a matier of law. [It is very important to understand the standard for the rule because the standard differs among the rules.]

Assuming the case has not settled, the parties will go to trial where they will call witnesses, present evidence, and make arguments. Each court has its own rules on the procedure for trials and what the parties must do before trail. Surprisingly, first-year classes generally do not talk much about trials.

If you lose at trial how do you appeal? This is important because there are specific mechanisms for appealing, and these mechanisms affect the cases you will read. Generally, litigants have to give the trial court a chance to correct its mistakes, and you appeal from the denial of these motions. The two main ways to allow a trial court to correct its errors are 1) a motion for a new trial and 2) a motion for judgment notwithstanding a verdict. To make a a motion for judgment notwithstanding the verdict, a party must have made a motion for a judgment as a matter of law (motion for directed verdict) during the trial. Here is the federal rule on these motions:

Rule 50. Judgment as a Matter of Law.

(1) In General. If a party has been fully heard on an issue during a jury trial

and the court finds <u>that a reasonable jury would not have a legally sufficient evidentiary basis to find for the party on that issue</u>, the court may:

(A) resolve the issue against the party; and

(B) grant a motion for judgment as a matter of law against the party on a claim or defense that, under the controlling law, can be maintained or defeated only with a favorable finding on that issue.

(2) Motion. A motion for judgment as a matter of law may be made at any time before the case is submitted to the jury. The motion must specify the judgment sought and the law and facts that entitle the movant to the judgment.

(b) Renewing the Motion After Trial; Alternative Motion for a New Trial. If the court does not grant a motion for judgment as a matter of law made under Rule 50(a), the court is considered to have submitted the action to the jury subject to the court's later deciding the legal questions raised by the motion. No later than 28 days after the entry of judgment—or if the motion addresses a jury issue not decided by a verdict, no later than 28 days after the jury was discharged—the movant may file a renewed motion for judgment as a matter of law and may include an alternative or joint request for a new trial under Rule 59. In ruling on the renewed motion, the court may:

(1) allow judgment on the verdict, if the jury returned a verdict;

(2) order a new trial; or

(3) direct the entry of judgment as a matter of law.

Note that I underlined the standard for a motion notwithstanding the verdict.

I'm going to stop here because I know that the above is a lot to take in. You will learn the excruciating details in Civil Procedure. The important thing to understand now is that each case you will read in law school involves one or more of these procedures and that the procedure determines the grounds for how a court will consider the procedure.

Exercises

Context for Law School

1. How does a litigant commence a lawsuit?
2. What is a summons?
3. What is a complaint?
4. How does a defendant respond to a complaint?
5. What is an answer?
6. What are the alternatives to filing an answer? Why do they exist?
7. What happens after the filing of an answer?
8. What are the main types of discovery?
9. What is a motion for a summary judgment? What is the standard for granting a motion for a summary judgment?
10. How does a litigant appeal an unfavorable judgment?
11. What is the purpose of appellate courts?
12. What is the standard for a motion notwithstanding the verdict?
13. Why is understanding procedure important for reading cases?

Note

1. When arguing to a judge do not use terms like reasoning by analogy or after synthesizing the cases. The judge will know what you are doing.

Chapter Eight
Wellness

Chapter Goals.

1. To stress the importance of wellness in law school.
2. To give you some things to do if you start to feel stress in law school.
3. To talk about drug and alcohol abuse.
4. To tell you what to do if things become overwhelming–immediately seek help!

As I have mentioned several times throughout this book, law school success involves a lot of effort. Nothing wrong with that; hard work is good for you. Unfortunately, law school also involves a lot of stress, and this stress can lead to depression, anxiety, alcoholism, and drug use. Here is the problem revealed by a survey of law students: "nearly one-quarter of the surveyed law students reported binge-drinking twice or more in the prior two weeks; more than one-third of respondents screened positive for moderate or severe anxiety; and roughly one-sixth screened positive for depression."[1] More importantly, "[f]rom July 2014 through February 2015, there were seven law student suicides and one law professor suicide."[2] In addition, "Stress harms our cardiovascular and immune systems, and exposure to chronic stress impairs learning and memory."[3]

These problems are why many law school are adopting "wellness" programs to help their students with the psychological pressures of a legal education. Before I talk about the details, if you are feeling overwhelmed in law school talk to someone. All law schools have a professional who is trained to deal with both students' academic and mental health problems. At most law schools, this person is called the dean of students. The dean of students may not be able to treat your specific problem, but this person will know where to send you within the university for help. Some law schools have on-site counselors, while others use university counseling centers.[4] Finally, some law schools have on-line surveys to check if you think you might need help.[5]

Repeat after me: I am not in this alone.

Here is one law school's introduction to stress and wellness :

"Stress is a physical and emotional reaction to a perceived threat – whether the threat exists or not. Our bodies go into 'fight or flight' mode as if we were faced with a saber-toothed tiger in early human days. In our modern lives, <u>our bodies and minds perceive smaller difficulties</u> (exams, arguments, busy schedules) <u>as major threats</u> – it's what we've evolved to do! But the good news is that we can learn to undo this unnecessary 'fight or flight' reaction using mindfulness-based skills. Managing our stress can have a direct impact on the quality of our sleep. And better sleep means less stress!"[6]

The first thing you need to understand about law school is that all students struggle at the beginning and all students feel some stress. Law school is something new for everyone. All law students are novices. No one goes from being a novice to an expert in a day, a week, a month, or even a year. You were probably the smartest student in the class at your university. However, now you know nothing–nothing. You are starting at the very beginning (which is a very good place to start). Your law professors don't expect you to be a genius. Also, talk to second and third years who can tell you about their first-year experiences.

The same is true for stress and mild anxiety. <u>When something is new, it is stressful.</u> We all fear the unknown. Similarly, newness gets us out of our comfort zone, which is good.

<u>You need help, however, when stress and anxiety get out of hand.</u>[7] You need help when you suffer mood changes. You need help when you start skipping classes. You need help when you start relying on drugs or alcohol. (I know of several students who flunked out of law school because of drug or alcohol problems. Drugs and alcohol have a strong negative effect on academic performance.) You need help when you start having problems sleeping. You have problems if you start to feel anti-social.

First, let's start with some simple things that will help you avoid the problems in the above paragraph. Law school is a lot of work, but you shouldn't overdo it (become obsessed). Slow and steady wins the race. Do a little bit of work everyday, rather than trying to cram a semester's worth of studying into one or two days. Get plenty of sleep, and eat regularly.[8] If you have a routine keep up that routine. For example, if you jog, don't suddenly stop jogging. (Actually, aerobic exercise is good for your brain, so everyone should exercise some.)[9] Don't increase your intake of alcohol or start taking drugs. If drinking has not been a problem in the past, you can keep drinking, but cut down a little and don't drink when you have important things the next day. Rely on your friends and family; they are there to help you. Finally, as I stressed above, realize that your classmates are going through what you are going through.

Many law schools recommend practicing mindfulness. "Mindfulness, the art of focusing on the present moment, can inspire emotion regulation, which benefits the person practicing self-control and the persons she interacts with."[10] One author recommends reappraisal: "People who learn reappraisal, a technique for reinterpreting a situation in order to transform its emotional meaning, can change the evaluation of the situation. Reappraisal, also called reframing, is learning to actively challenge negative interpretations and find positive ways to interpret stressful situations."[11] Similarly, having a purpose and taking responsibility helps with wellness.[12] The same author recommends a strong social network of significant others, friends, mentors, and confidants."[13] Meditation also leads to mindfulness, as does "the loving-kindness technique of wishing others well" and expressing gratitude.[14] Likewise, use "visualization, where you use your imagination to think about who you want to become or what you hope to accomplish."[15] Important habits to avoid include comparing yourself to others and being a perfectionist.[16] Finally one website recommends 71 Mindfulness Exercises for Living in the Present Moment, including writing in a journal, connect with nature, decrease distractions, take a digital break, and engage in handwork.[17]

Many law schools offer wellness (or mindfulness) workshops. It is a good idea to attend these workshops even if you are not having problems. Preventative medicine is better than emergency surgery. Here are some on-line materials on stress relief, including stress relief exercises from Yale Law School. (https://yalehealth.yale.edu/more/stress-relief-relaxation-healthy-sleep)

Your attitude toward law school also affects your mental well-being. (I mentioned this is Chapter One). Many students think of law school as something they have to endure before they can make a living. Such an attitude makes law school a burden–a chore, rather than something you want to do, and it leads to the problems discussed in this chapter. Try to think of law school as an opportunity to learn. Similarly, extrinsic reasons for attending law school, such as parental pressure or just needing something to do, can lead to mental problems.

The key to successfully navigating law school without excessive stress is to draw on intrinsic factors. A law school wellness expert has asserted, "Those values and motivations that promote or attend professionalism have been empirically shown to correlate with well being and life satisfaction, while those that undermine or discourage professionalism empirically correlate with distress and dissatisfaction."[18] He continued, distinguishing intrinsic from extrinsic motivators, "The former values direct one towards self-understanding, close relationships with others, prosocial/helping out-comes, and community improvement, while the latter embody a more contingent worth, external rewards orientation–toward money, luxuries, influence and appearance." For example, "one is intrinsically motivated when he chooses an action which he genuinely enjoys or which furthers a fundamental life purpose, while extrinsically motivated choices are directed towards external rewards (i.e. money, grades, honors), avoidance of guilt or fear, or pleasing/impressing others." He argued that an attorneys' "life experience[s] will be enhanced on many levels if they model the wise, compassionate lawyer-statesperson." He added, "Empirical research for the past two decades has consistently shown that intrinsic values and motivation, when primary in a person's value system, produce satisfaction and well-being, whereas when extrinsic values and motivation are primary they produce angst and distress." (Doesn't the above sound a lot like my discussion of motivation earlier in this book? In both cases, intrinsic factors are more effective than extrinsic ones.)

The same professor added, "Real professionalism engenders a sense of competence, self-respect, and respect for and from others, as well as imbuing one's work with meaning and providing that sense of authenticity (integrity) that we have raised earlier." He also noted, "Selfish, superficial goals and values strip work of its potential for meaning, leaving an emptiness that can breed a compulsion for more work (and money) or other addictive traits."

More specifically, Professors Krieger and Sheldon have studied the factors that contribute to lawyer happiness.[19] They note that "all human beings have certain basic psychological needs—to feel competent/effective, autonomous/authentic, and related/connected with others."

Their article concluded:

1. "Objective factors that often dominate the attention of law students and lawyers (and legal employersand teachers as well)—law school grade performance, law review membership, law school debt, and income after graduation—[] only modestly predict attorney well-being and [] therefore provide a contrast when compared to the expected stronger associations with well-being of the internal factors included in the study."

2. "The frequency of experiences of autonomy (which includes authenticity),

competence, and relatedness to other people [] very strongly predict lawyer well-being."

3. "The extent to which subjects' motivation for their work was internal (for interest, enjoyment, and meaning), rather than external (for money, status, or prestige, or imposed by others), []also strongly predict[s] well-being."

4. "Lawyers who more strongly endorsed intrinsic values (for growth, intimacy, community, and altruism) to be happier than those who more strongly endorsed extrinsic values (for affluence, status, fame, and appearance)."

5. "Attorneys who receive[] autonomy-supportive—as opposed to controlling—supervision [] thrive to a substantially greater extent than others."

In sum, "Human beings also have a deep-rooted and fundamental desire for meaning in terms of making sense of their lives."[20] Now, can you see why going to law school for only extrinsic reasons can result in mental problems?

Recently, many legal ethics experts, including the author of this book, have talked about the importance of law students developing their professional identities, while in law school.[21] Professional identity is "what it means to be a lawyer in today's world."[22] It "is the way a lawyer understands his or her role relative to all of the stakeholders in the legal system, including clients, courts, opposing parties and counsel, the firm, and even the legal system itself (or society as a whole)."[23] Professional identity is more than knowing how to apply ethical rules. It is personal; it involves the inner you (your moral compass). It is "a process of human development."[24]

How does a law student develop his or her professional identity? Books have been written on this topic, including the one of mine I mentioned in the endnotes. However, let me give you an introduction to developing your professional identity.

First, you reflect on who you want to be as a lawyer. (Have you noticed how many times I have suggested you reflect on something in the book?)

Sample Reflection Questions

1. Who do I want to be as a lawyer? How does this relate to my personality? My morality? What do I want to accomplish in life?
2. How do I get there?
3. What area of law do I want to practice in? How does this fit with the questions in question 1?

4. Do you think representing the poor and disadvantaged would be satisfying? What are the downsides to this type of practice?

5. Do you want to represent corporations? Why or why not?

6. What do you think the following lawyers do in a common day: 1) a big law attorney, 2) a general practitioner, 3) an estate attorney, 4) a torts plaintiffs lawyer, 5) a torts defense lawyer, 6) a corporate attorney, 7) a criminal defense attorney, 8) a prosecutor, 9) an in-house attorney at a big corporation, 10) an attorney who drafts documents, 11) a real estate attorney, 12) a judge, 13) a government attorney? Do any of these areas interest you?

7. Is it okay to overstate your billable hours if your job is in jeopardy?

8. How do you want others to view you as a lawyer?

9. What is more important–your reputation or making a lot of money?

10. Would you rather be viewed as an aggressive attorney or a civil one?

11. Your client wants you to "beat up on the otherside." You don't think that this will give you any advantage in winning the case. What do you do? (Assume the client will be in court.)

Second, it is important to see how attorneys act. Do you have any friends who will mentor you? If not, attend a session of a court and observe how attorneys act. Do you think some attorneys are more professional than others? Can bad attorney behavior negatively affect the judge? (The answer to this last question is yes. I saw it happen many times when I was an attorney.)

Professor Krieger has created an exercise to emphasize the above points: He has students write down what they think their eulogy would be when given by a relative or friend.[25] He points out, "The results of this exercise are illuminating, because they invariably show students and lawyers the kinds of things that matter to them in the deepest way. It turns out that the qualities and values typically expressed in these eulogies are the most traditional human values and virtues: patience, decency, humility, courage, caring, integrity, willingness to work hard for worthwhile goals, helpfulness to others (family, friends, clients or community), and so forth. No one thus far in my experience has drafted a eulogy about a luxurious home, high grade point average or exceptionally lucrative law practice."

Professor Krieger concluded, "If you focus your life on gaining wealth, popularity, prestige, or influence, you are making a mistake (assuming you want to feel satisfied with your life). If you focus your life on growth, integrity, compassion and respectfulness on the levels of your self (which includes honoring your values and heeding your conscience), your personal and professional relationships, and your community interactions–your life will feel meaningful and satisfying. You will avoid the frustration, isolation, emptiness, compulsions and addictions common to many in our society and our profession. And as a side benefit, you will also undoubtedly grow in comforts beyond your needs, because your right choices will create positive outcomes and good will."

Now, let's talk about what to do if your stress and anxiety problems become serious. I have only one piece of advice on this one (which I've previously given): talk to a professional at your law school as soon as possible. (Or your doctor, if you have one.) Why only this advice? Because no book can help you deal with serious mental health or substance abuse problems. None.

Many students with serious problems do not seek help: "For instance, while forty-two percent of the surveyed law students reported that they believed they required help for emotional or mental health issues in the past year, only half of those students actually sought assistance from a mental health professional. Equally concerning, although twenty-five percent of students reported behavior indicative of problematic drinking, only four percent indicated that they had ever received counseling for substance use issues."[26]

There is no stigma for getting help for mental health problems. Mental health problems are just like physical health problems. You wouldn't ignore pneumonia would you? Most importantly, counseling is confidential; your friends won't know you are going unless you tell them. (Which actually is a good idea. Friends provide comfort.)

Questions: Your Well-Being

1. Professors Ryff and Keyes write that well-being consists of 1) self-acceptance, 2) environmental mastery, 3) purpose in life, 4) positive relations with others, 5) personal growth, and 6) autonomy.[27] Rate yourself on each of these factors from 1 to 10.
2. Why did you decide to become a lawyer?
3. Do you enjoy law school?
4. What do you like the most about law school? What do you like the least? (be specific)
5. How has law school affected your emotional well-being? How?
6. Do you think the area of law you have chosen will be satisfying? Why?

7. What do you look forward to about being a lawyer? Writing briefs? Arguing in court? Meeting with clients? Doing business planning?

8. Do you have any doubts about being a lawyer? How do these doubts affect your current well-being?

9. Are your motivations in law school intrinsic, or extrinsic, or both? (be specific)

10. How can you better develop your intrinsic motivators?

11. Do you like working with people? How does this relate to your chosen area of law?

12. Do you prefer to work alone? How does this relate to your chosen area of law?

13. Do you like helping others? How does this relate to your chosen area of law? Do you want to do pro bono when you become a lawyer?

14. Do you like intellectual things? How does this relate to your chosen area of law?

15. What gives you satisfaction? What gives your life meaning?

16. Did you pick college courses because they were interesting, because they would help you in your career, or because they were easy? Did you do better in classes you thought were interesting?

17. Why is lawyer well-being important to clients? Why is lawyer well-being important to employers?

18. What are your strengths, and how do they relate to your chosen area of law?

19. What are your weaknesses, and how will they affect your chosen area of law?

20. On a scale of 1 to 10 with 10 being the highest, rate your well-being before you went to law school.

21. Rate your well-being now.

22. List the ways that law school has affected your well-being.

23. Do you take time for yourself?

23. Do you exercise?

24. Do you take time to be with friends? Do you talk about your problems with your friends?

25. Are you depressed? Do you have trouble sleeping? Do you drink too much? Use drugs?

26. Is there any thing wrong with seeing a counselor when you need one?

27. Have you ever considered joining a self-help group?

28. I one had a friend many years ago who said he could never enjoy himself unless he was drunk or high? Do you think he succeeded at life?

Wellness

There are no right answers to these questions. Also, if you are just starting law school, you may not be able to answer some of these questions yet.

Notes

1. Debra S. Austin, Windmills of Your Mind: Understanding the Neurobiology of Emotion, https://papers.ssrn.com/sol3/papers.cfm?abstract_id=3374006 (2019).

2. *Id.*

3. *Id.*

4. Jordana Alter Confino, *Where Are We on the Path to Law Student Well-Being?: Report on the ABA CoLAP Law Student Assistance Committee Law School Wellness Survey*, https://papers.ssrn.com/sol3/papers.cfm?abstract_id=3374976 at 5-8 (2019).

5. *E.g.*, https://www.hazeldenbettyford.org/treatment/admissions/assessments; https://www.law.miami.edu/students/wellness-resources.

6. https://yalehealth.yale.edu/more/stress-relief-relaxation-healthy-sleep.

7. "[W]hen we experience chronic long-term stress due to family demands, financial problems, or workplace issues, the stress response fails to turn off." Austin, *supra*.

8. In addition, lack of sleep impairs learning. "Much of memory processing occurs while we sleep, making adequate sleep very important to the learning process. Getting a sufficient amount of sleep is critical to thinking and learning because sleep deprivation impairs 'attention, executive function, working memory, mood, quantitative skills, logical reasoning ability, general math knowledge,' and manual dexterity. Habits that can interfere with sleep include ingesting caffeine late in the day, the intake of nicotine and alcohol, and the use of digital media too close to bed time." Austin, *supra*.

9. *Id.*

10. *Id.*

11. *Id.*

12. *Id.*

13. *Id.*

14. *Id.*

15. *Id.*

16. *Id.*

17. https://www.developgoodhabits.com/mindfulness-exercises/.

18. Lawrence S. Krieger, *The Inseparability of Professionalism and Personal Satisfaction*, http://papers.ssrn.com/sol3/papers.cfm?abstract_id=549361&download=yes at 5 (2004).

19. Lawrence S. Krieger & Kennon M. Sheldon, What Makes Lawyers Happy?: A Data-Driven Prescription to Redefine Professional Success, http://papers.ssrn.com/sol3/papers.cfm?abstract_id=239898 (2015).

20. Peter H. Huang & Rick Swedloff, Authentic Happiness and Meaning at Law Firms, http://www.researchgate.net/profile/Peter_Huang5/publication/228222844_Authentic_Happiness_and_Meaning_at_Law_Firms/links/02e7e521ae84a92256000000.pdf at 5 (2008).

21. E. SCOTT FRUEHWALD, DEVELOPING YOUR PROFESSIONAL IDENTITY: CREATING YOUR INNER LAWYER (2015).

22. Roberto L. Corrada & David Thomson, Report on the 2012 Conference and Introduction to the 2013 Conference: The Development of Professional Identity in Legal Education: Rethinking Learning and Assessment, at *2 (Educating Tomorrow's Lawyers 2013).

23. Martin J. Katz, Teaching Professional Identity in Law School, 42 Colo. Lawyer 45, 45 (2013).

24. Michael J. Cedrone, The Developmental Path of the Lawyer, 41 Cap. U. L. Rev. 779, 782 (2013).

25. Krieger at 2.

26. Confino, *supra* at 5, n. 11.

27. See Carol D. Ryff & Corey Lee M. Keyes, The Structure of Psychological Well-Being Revisited, 69 J. Personality & Soc. Psych. 720 (1995).

CPSIA information can be obtained
at www.ICGtesting.com
Printed in the USA
FSHW021943150819
61106FS